Janelle Ho and Helen Pearson

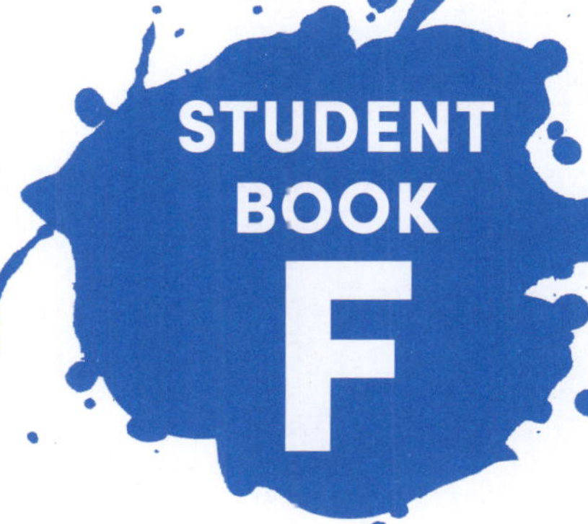

Australian Curriculum Edition

Name: ______________________

Class: ______________________

Spelling Rules! Student Book F
Australian Curriculum Edition
ISBN: 978 0 6550 9266 7

Designer and typesetter: Trish Hayes
Illustrator: Stephen Michael King
Series editor: Marie James
Indigenous consultant: Al Fricker

This edition published in 2024 by **Matilda Education Australia**, an imprint of Meanwhile Education Pty Ltd
PO Box 118, Burwood, Victoria, Australia 3125
T: 1300 277 235
E: customersupport@matildaed.com.au
W: www.matildaeducation.com.au

First edition published in 2006 by Macmillan Science and Education Australia Pty Ltd

Printed in China by Central
Sep-2023

NOTE TO TEACHERS AND PARENTS

Spelling Rules!

Some students are natural spellers. But the vast majority of students need formal, systematic and sequential instruction about the way spelling works and the strategies they can use to become independent, confident spellers and spelling risk-takers.

The *Spelling Rules!* program is based on sound linguistic and pedagogical theory. It is informed by research into how students of different ages acquire and apply spelling skills, and how those skills move from the working to the long-term memory. The program closely follows the Australian English curriculum. *Australian Curriculum: English* references are provided in the Teacher Resource Books. The program consists of seven student books, fully supported by two Teacher Resource Books.

Each student book contains units of work, with each unit designed to be used over the course of a week. The content of each unit simultaneously develops new skills and reinforces skills from previous units. The introduction of new sounds and letter patterns is logically sequenced and takes into account both frequency of use and complexity. Where appropriate, topic words from other curriculum areas such as mathematics, science and social sciences are included. When spelling rules are introduced, only known sounds and letter patterns are used so that students focus on one skill at a time. Regular revision units enable teachers to assess student progress and reinforce key rules and patterns from previous units.

Spelling knowledge

Learning to spell involves developing different kinds of spelling knowledge:

- **Kinaesthetic knowledge** – the physical feeling when saying different sounds and words, and when writing the shapes of letters and words
- **Phonological knowledge** – how a word sounds and the patterns of sounds in words
- **Visual knowledge** – how letters and words look and the visual patterns in words
- **Morphemic knowledge** – the meaning or function of words or parts of words
- **Etymological knowledge** – the origins and history of words and the effect this has on spelling patterns.

Icons used in Student Book F

The following icons identify the main spelling strategy that students will use to complete an activity.

Say the word. (Kinaesthetic knowledge) These activities ask students to experience how sounds feel in the mouth and jaw. Changing the positions of the jaw, lips, and tongue changes the sounds we make. Encourage students to pronounce the sounds and words accurately. If they mispronounce a sound or word, they may misrepresent it in writing.

Listen to the word. (Phonological knowledge) These activities focus on discriminating between different sounds and breaking up words into syllables or individual sound segments (phonemes).

Look at the word. (Visual knowledge) These activities help students to see how the sound is represented using combinations of letters, and to associate this visual pattern with what they are hearing. Students will develop the ability to know when a word does or does not 'look right'.

Understand the word. (Morphemic and etymological knowledge) These activities focus on word meanings, word families, prefixes and suffixes, spelling rules, word origins and so on – all of which help embed spelling in the long-term memory.

Practise writing the word. (Kinaesthetic knowledge) These activities develop students' awareness of the physical movement involved in writing the word. By practising writing the word a number of times and in different contexts, the spelling becomes embedded in the long-term memory.

This icon highlights useful spelling rules.

This icon tells students that a special clue or hint is provided for an activity. It may be a spelling, grammar or punctuation convention, or a definition of a useful term.

Spelling Rules! Student Book F (ISBN 9780655092667) © Janelle Ho, Helen Pearson

Student Book F

Units of work

The third edition of *Student Book F* contains 32 weekly units of work. You would probably start using the workbook towards the end of term 1 of the first year at school, once other routines are settled. Each unit focuses on one or more consonants or vowels. These letters are grouped according to how easily students are able to distinguish them by sight and by sound. In this revised edition, high-frequency sight words are introduced at an earlier stage, from Unit 5. Common digraphs and the simple suffix s are taught. See the **Scope and Sequence** chart on the inside front cover for more information.

Word lists

From Unit 3 onwards, there is a short word list for each unit. These core words have been chosen to support the learning focus and strategies being taught in the unit. The words contain the focus letter, letter pattern or morphological element. In addition, high-frequency words are introduced.

Spelling lists enable a particular rule, letter pattern, sound pattern, etymology or morphemic element to be focused on. There are sufficient examples to consolidate the teaching point. Additional words are provided in traceable letters. These words allow students to begin practising high-frequency sight words. By the end of *Student Book F* students will have been introduced to almost all the high-frequency sight words they need for reading and writing.

Unit at a glance

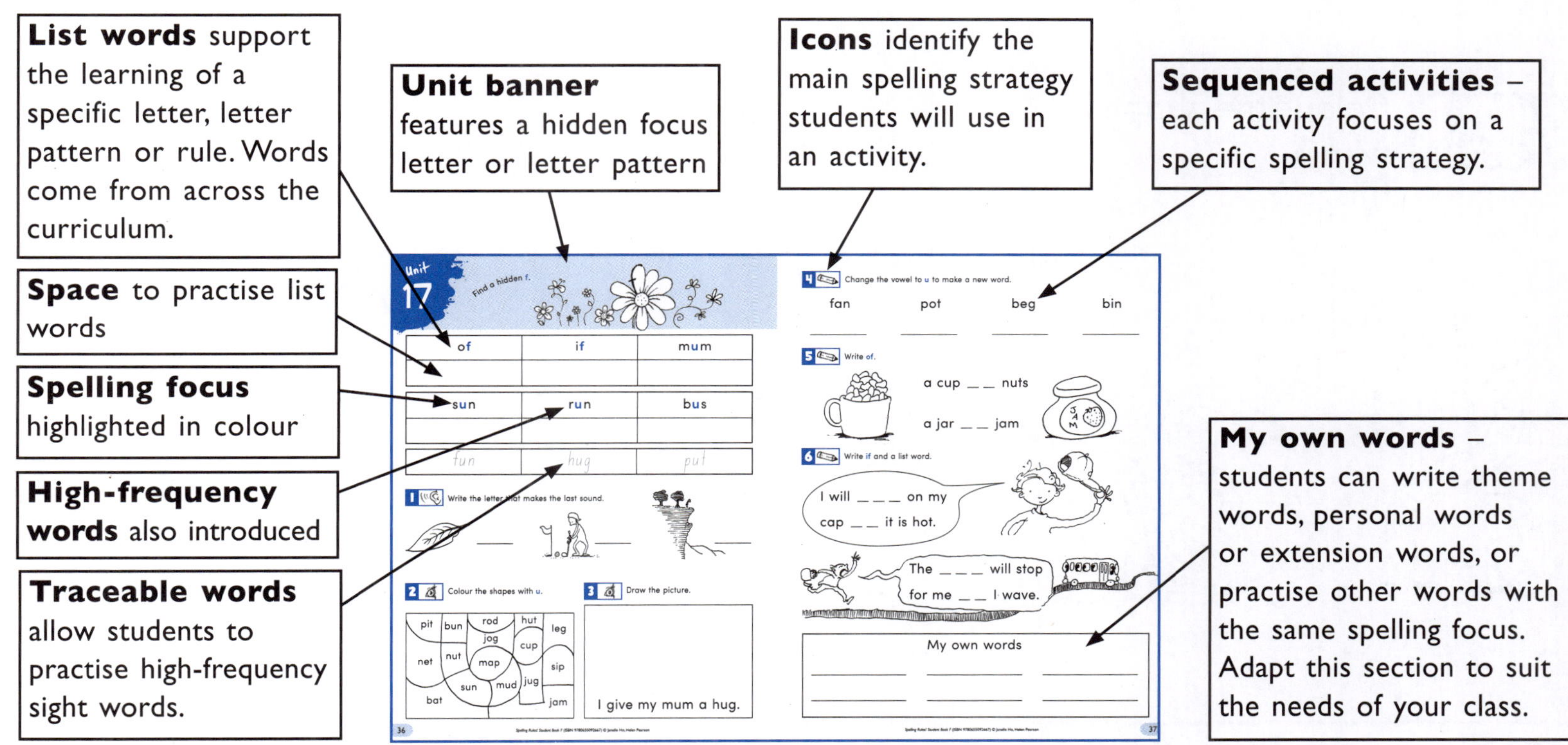

Spelling Rules! Teacher Resource Book F–2

Full teacher support for *Student Book F* is provided by *Spelling Rules! Teacher Resource Book F–2*. Here you will find valuable background information about spelling development and spelling knowledge, along with practical resources, such as:

- teaching tips for every unit in *Student Book F*
- extra word lists
- strategies for teaching spelling
- guidelines for assessing spelling and diagnosing spelling errors
- activities to support struggling spellers
- worthwhile extension for more able spellers.

Unit 1

Find a hidden **s**.

What letter can you see in the pictures? Write the letter.

____

____

2 Colour the shapes with **s**.
What do you see? ______

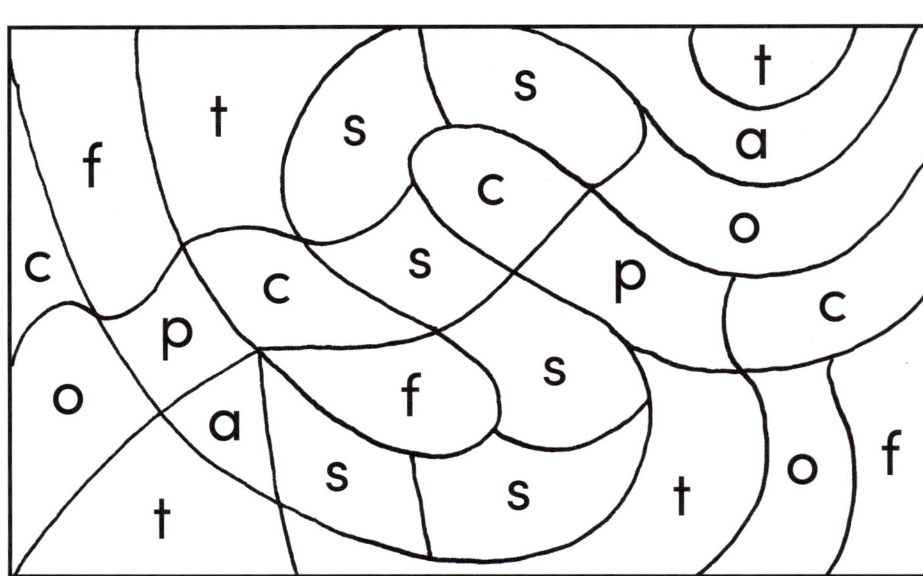

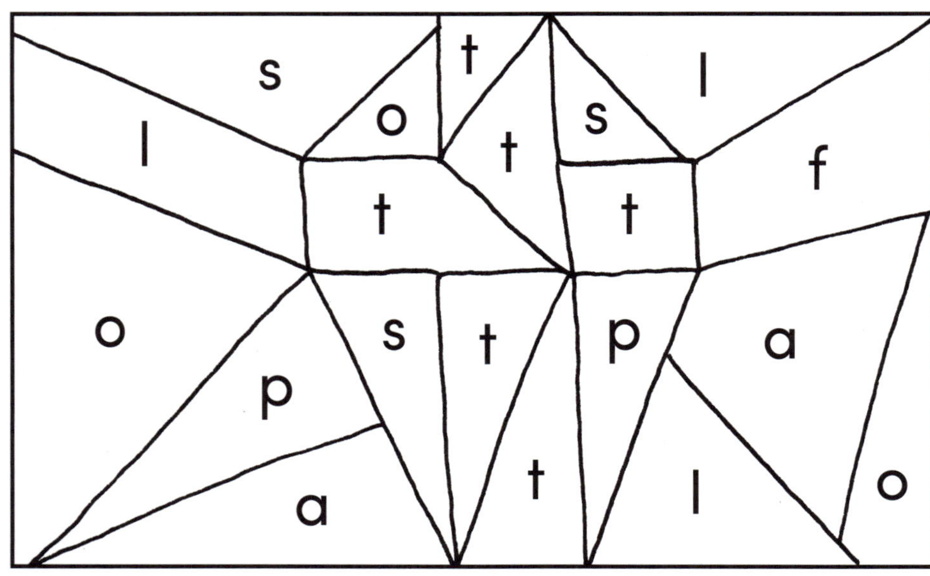

Colour the shapes with **t**.
What do you see?
_____

Spelling Rules! Student Book F (ISBN 9780655092667) © Janelle Ho, Helen Pearson

Write the letter that makes the first sound.

Draw a line to join the first sound to the picture.

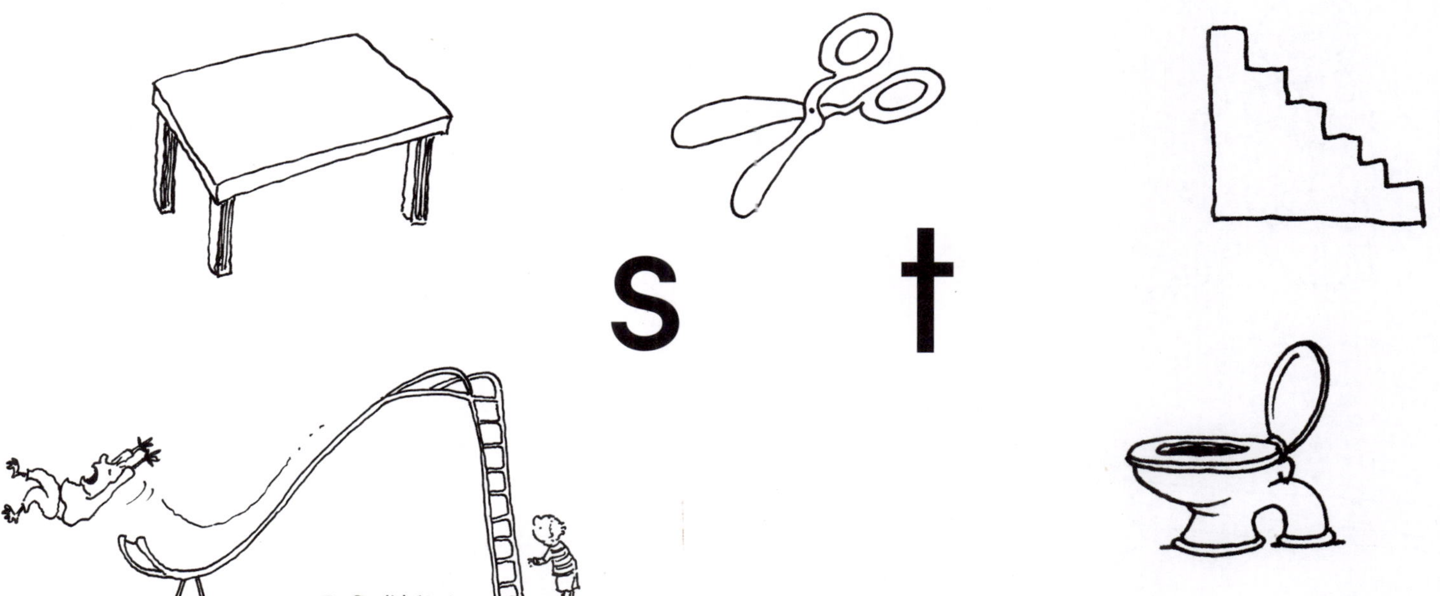

My own words

Unit 2

Find a hidden **a**.

1 What letter can you see in the pictures? Write the letter.

______

______

2 Circle the letter that makes the first sound.

a

p

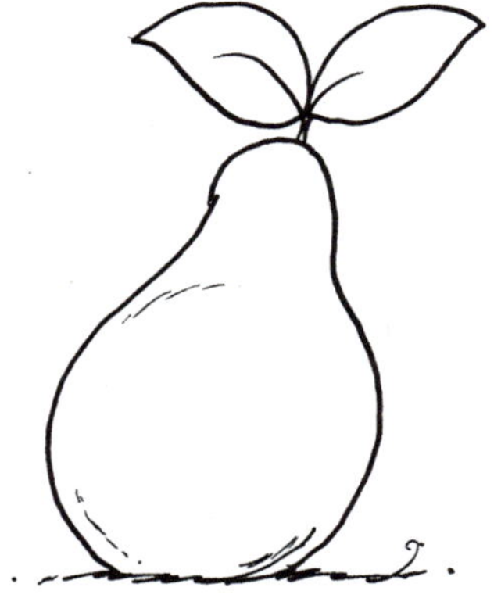

a

p

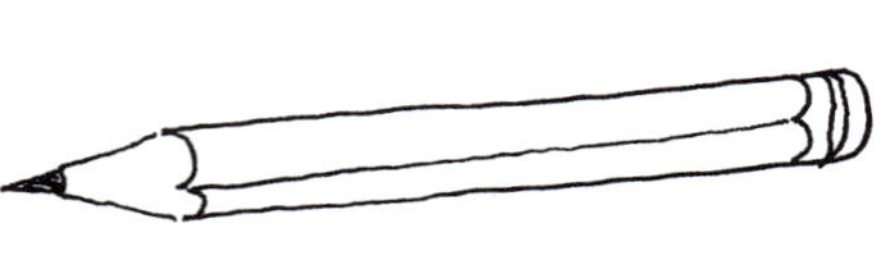

a

p

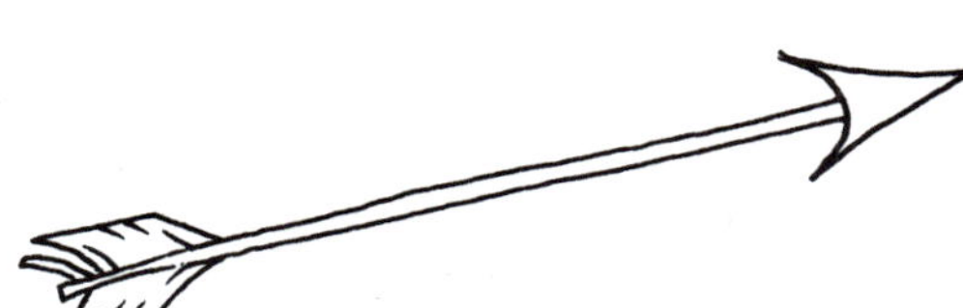

a

p

a

p

a

p

Spelling Rules! Student Book F (ISBN 9780655092667) © Janelle Ho, Helen Pearson

 Write the letter that makes the first sound.

 Write the letter **a** in each section of the shape.

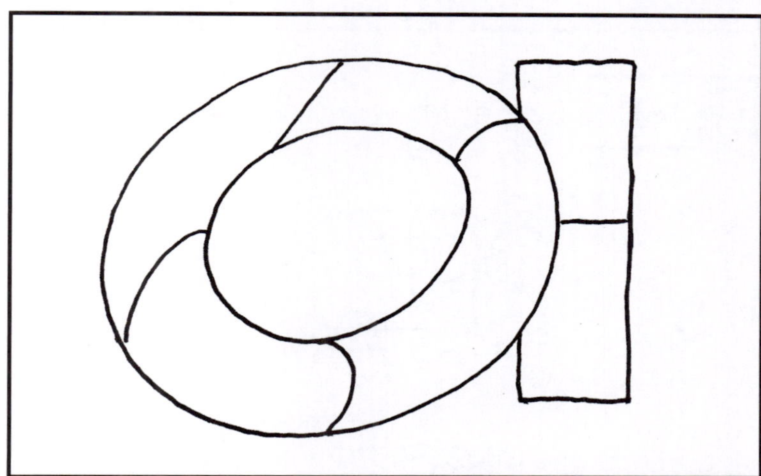

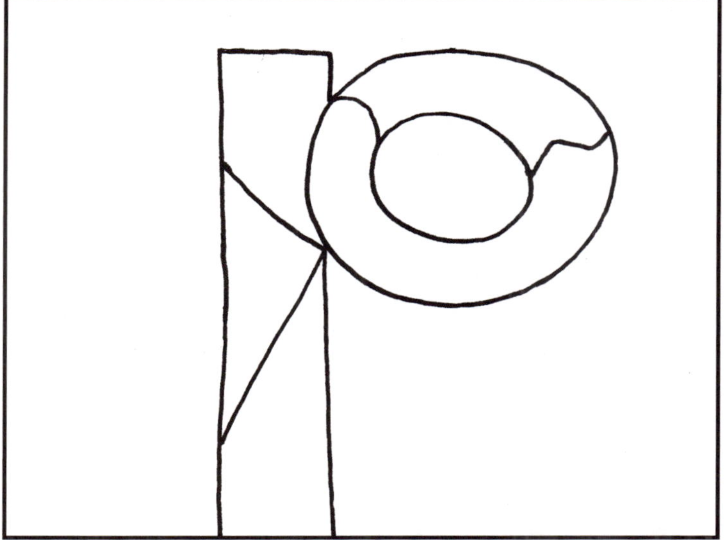

Write the letter **p** in each section of the shape.

My own words

Unit 3

Find a hidden t.

pat	sat	tap

1 Say each word. Write the last sound you hear.

s  ____  ____  ____

t  ____  ____  ____

p  ____  ____ 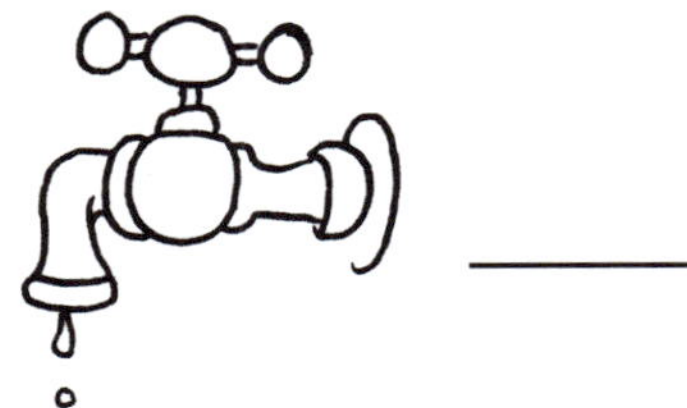 ____

2 Draw a line from the picture to the letter that makes the last sound.

p

s

t

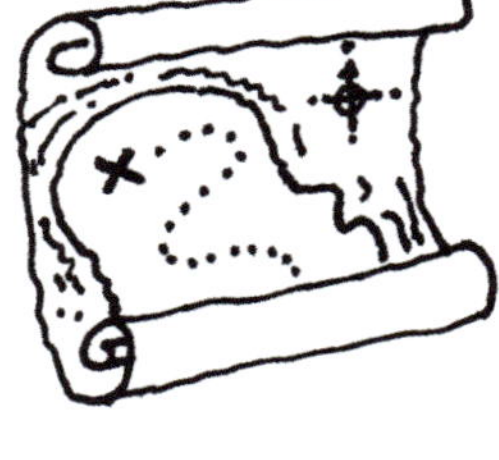

Spelling Rules! Student Book F (ISBN 9780655092667) © Janelle Ho, Helen Pearson

3 Colour **p** in blue. Colour **t** in red. Colour **a** in yellow. Colour **s** in green.

sat

4 Colour the picture if you hear **a** in the middle.

5 Write the missing letter.

r _ t

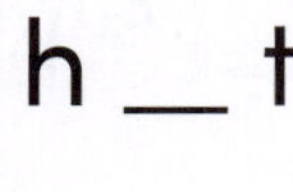

c _ t

m _ t

My own words

______________ ______________ ______________

______________ ______________ ______________

Unit 4

Find a hidden c.

cat	cap	gap

1 What letter can you see in the picture? Write the letter.

____

____

2 Say each word. Write the letter that makes the first sound.

____

____

c

____

____

____

____

g

____

____

Spelling Rules! Student Book F (ISBN 9780655092667) © Janelle Ho, Helen Pearson

3 Make words with different first sounds.

c
t → ap ______
g

______
______

p
s → at ______
c

______
______

4 Write list words.

I see a  in a 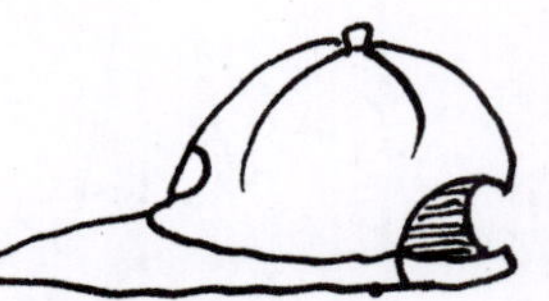

_ _ _   _ _ _

Sam's smile has a 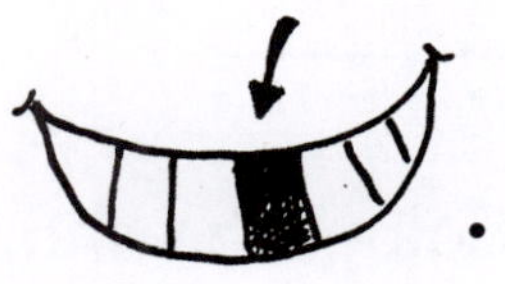.

_ _ _

My own words

______ ______ ______

______ ______ ______

Unit 5

Find a hidden m.

mat	map	it	is

sip	pit	in	a

Say the words. Write i or m for the first sound.

Colour the shapes with i.

What do you see?

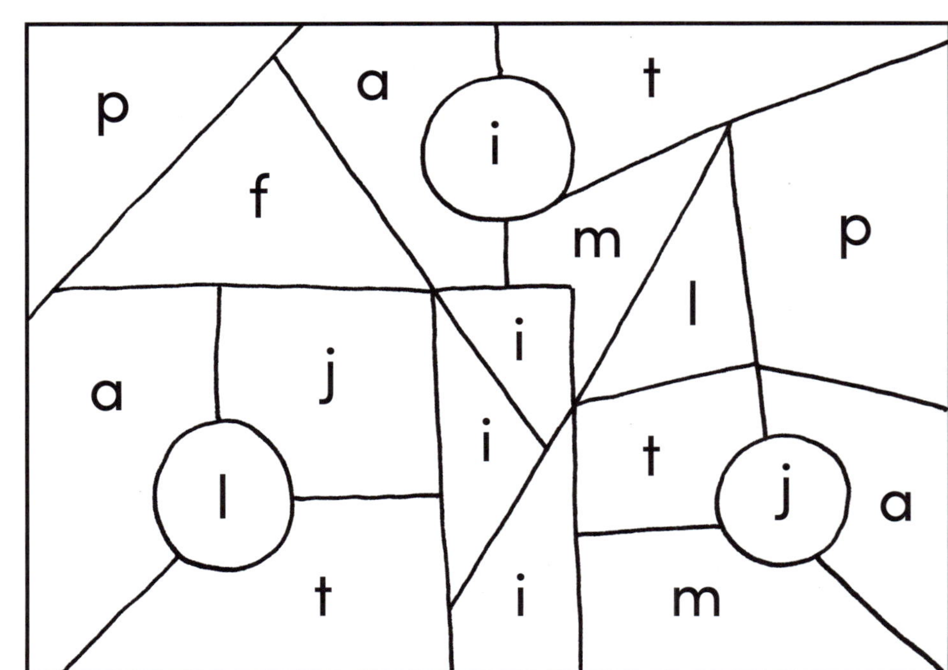

Spelling Rules! Student Book F (ISBN 9780655092667) © Janelle Ho, Helen Pearson

3 Write list words.

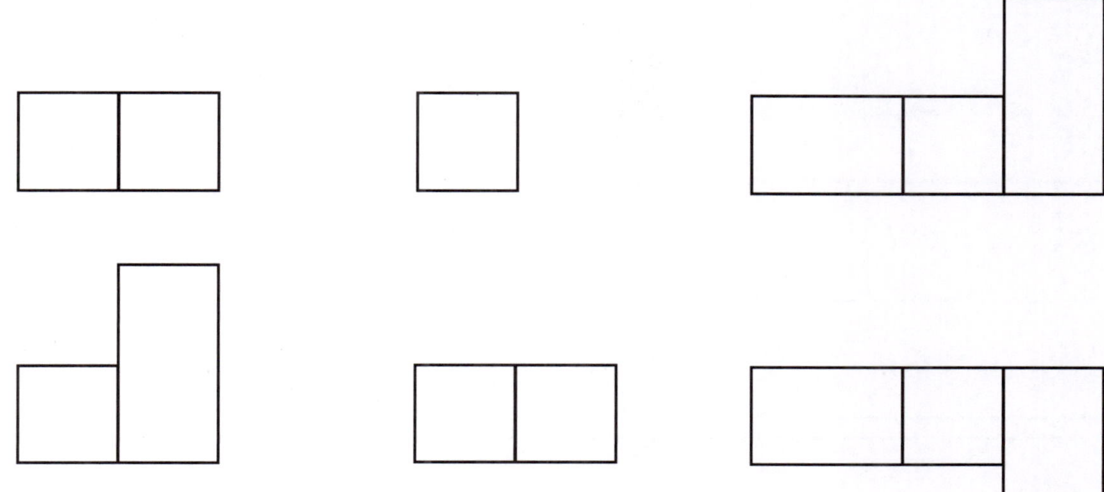

4  Write list words.

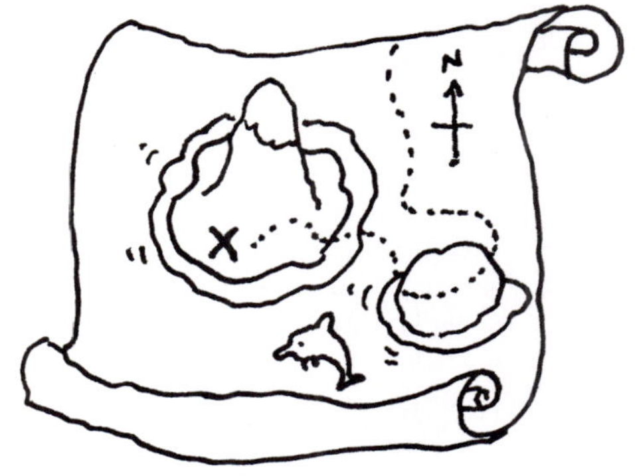

What is it?

It is a ___ ___ ___.

What is it?

It is a ___ ___ ___.

My own words

______________________ ______________________ ______________________

______________________ ______________________ ______________________

Unit 6

sit	pig	tip

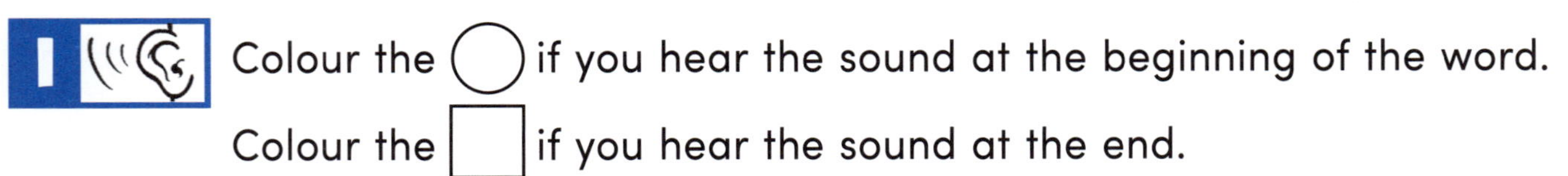

tag	am	at

1 Colour the ◯ if you hear the sound at the beginning of the word.
Colour the ☐ if you hear the sound at the end.

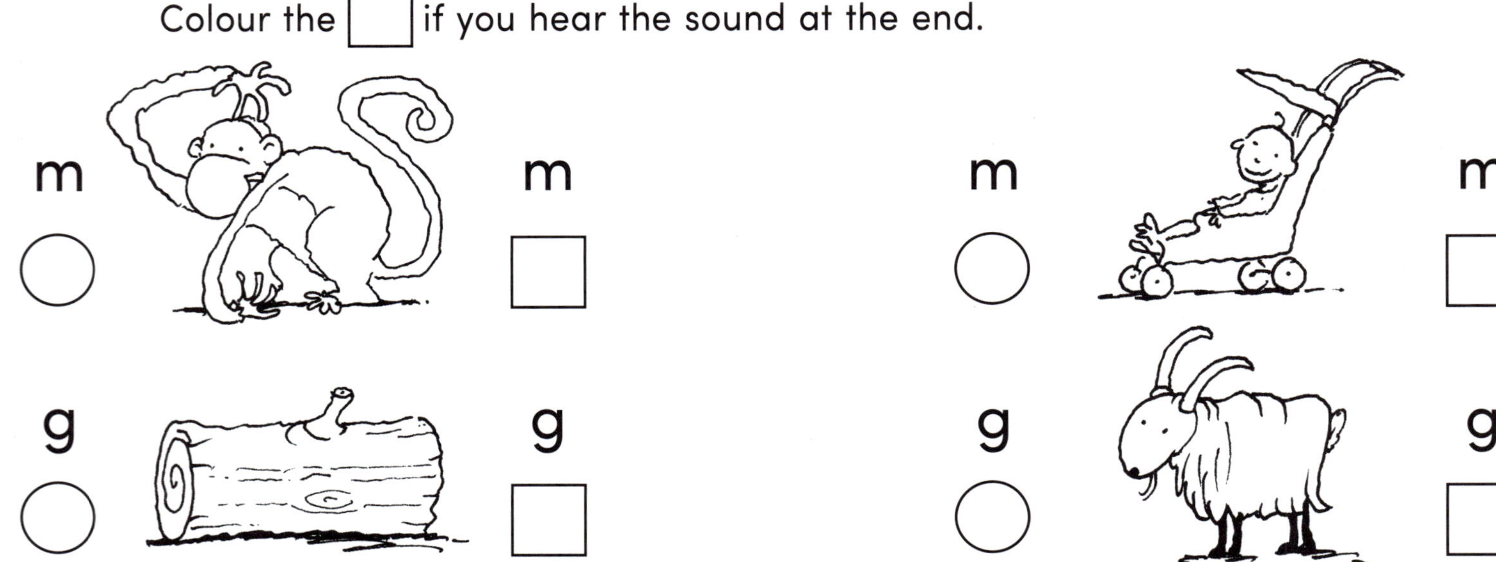

2 Write the letter that makes the last sound.

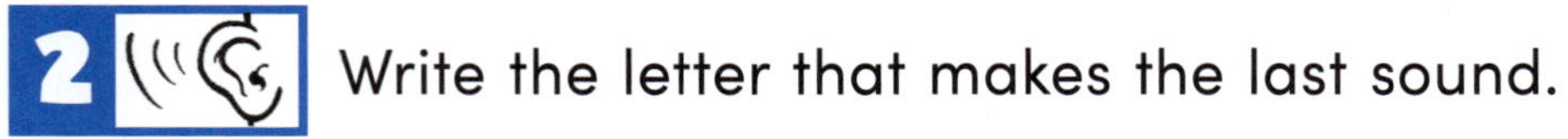

Spelling Rules! Student Book F (ISBN 9780655092667) © Janelle Ho, Helen Pearson

3 Say each word. Write **a** or **i**.

d _ g

s _ t

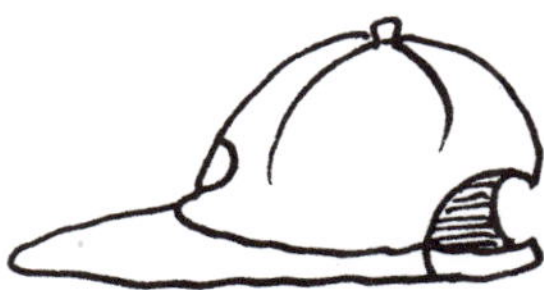

c _ p

r _ t

4 Write the missing letters.

I _ m Tim.

A p _ _ s _ ts on a m _ _.

Do not s _ _ on the t _ _ of a pin.

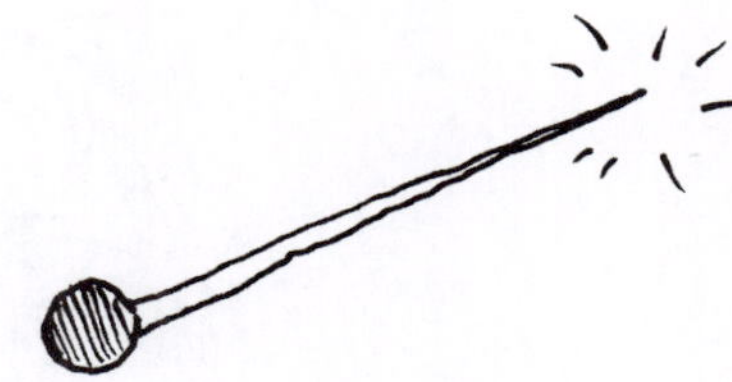

My own words		
______	______	______
______	______	______

Unit 7

Find a hidden l.

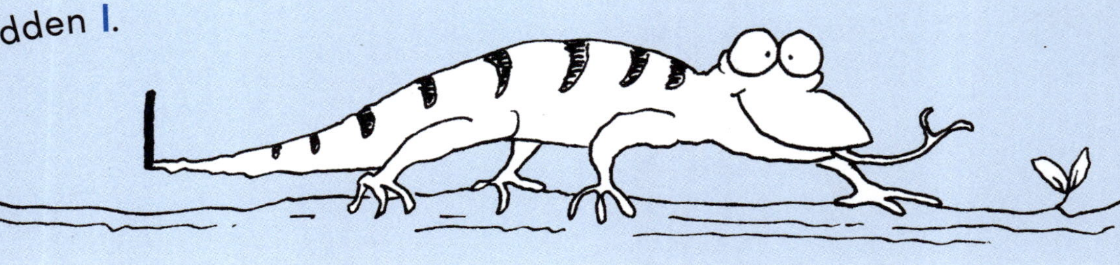

dig	lip	lap

dip	do	did

1 Colour the pictures starting with **d** red. Colour the pictures starting with **l** blue.

2 Write **d** or **l** for the first sound.

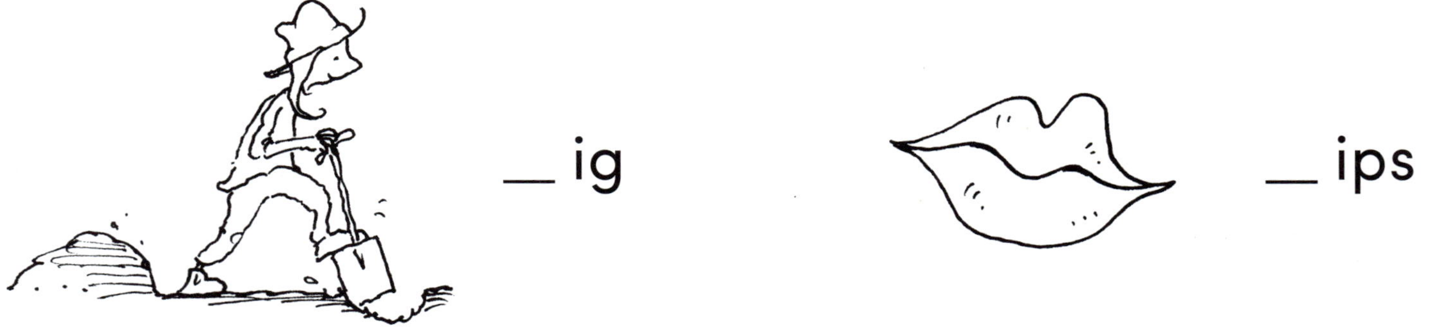

_ ig

_ ips

3 Draw lines to join the rhyming words.

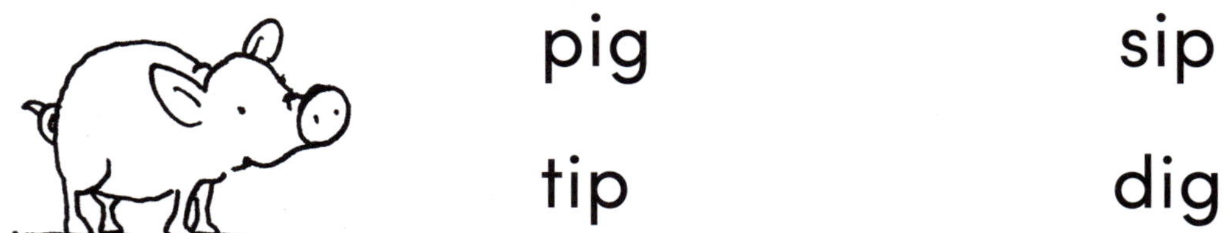

pig

tip

sip

dig

Spelling Rules! Student Book F (ISBN 9780655092667) © Janelle Ho, Helen Pearson

4 Make words with different first sounds.

d / p > ig ______ ______

l / s / t > ip ______ ______ ______

5 Make words with different last sounds.

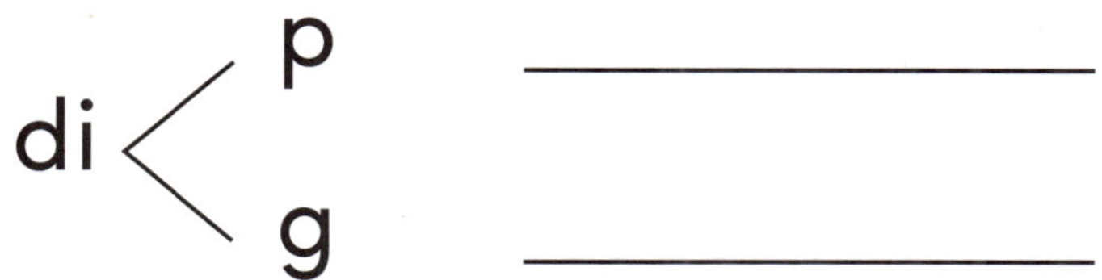

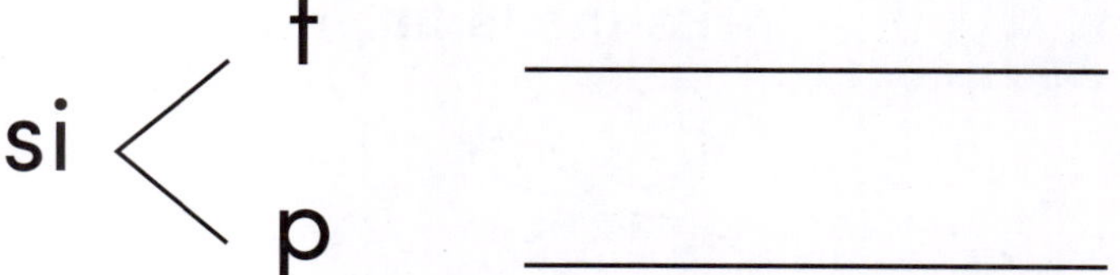

6 Change one letter to make a new word.

lap	______	sit	______
tap	______	pit	______
at	______	did	______

My own words

______ ______ ______

______ ______ ______

Unit 8

Find a hidden **n**.

no	**n**ap	**n**ip	**a**s

on	pal	cats	dogs

1 Write the letter that makes the first sound.

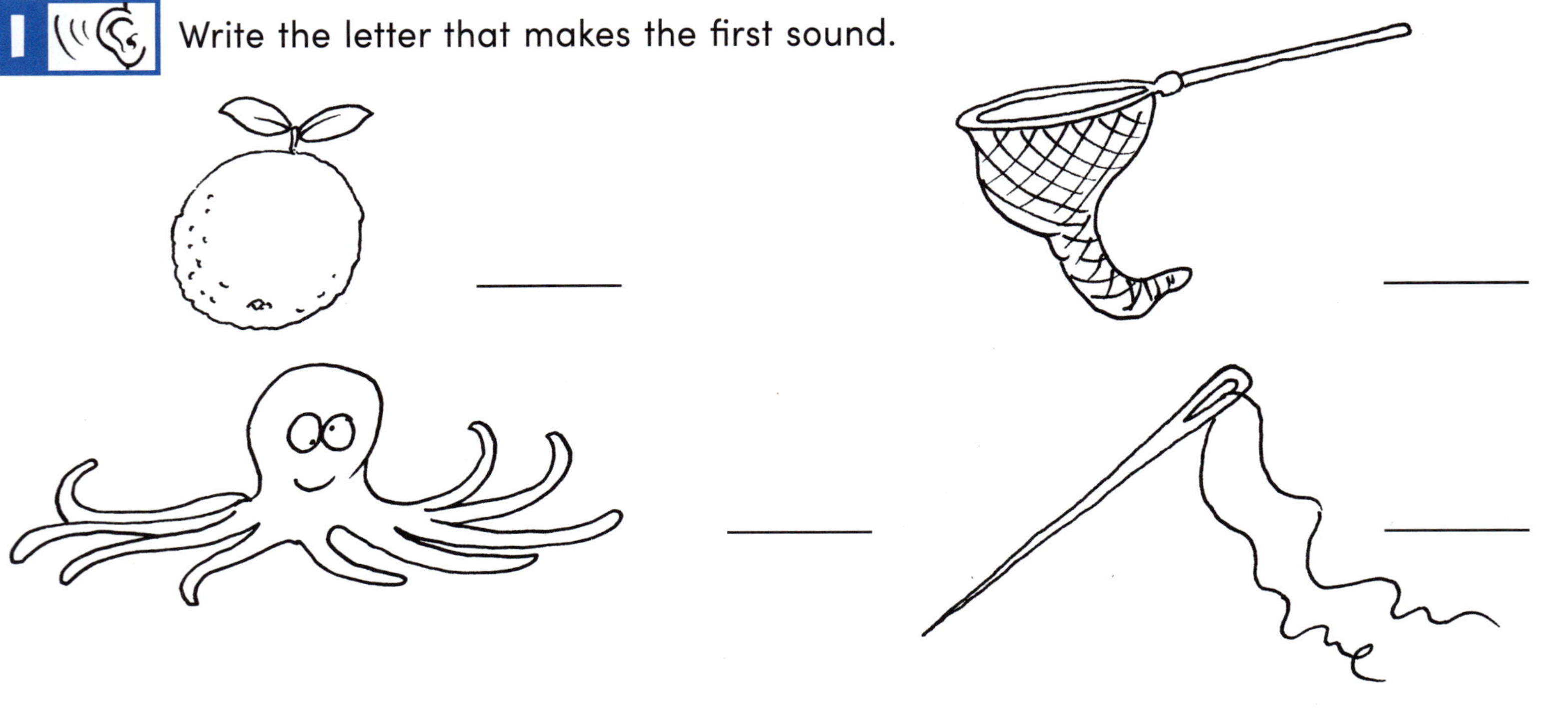

2 Write different list words.

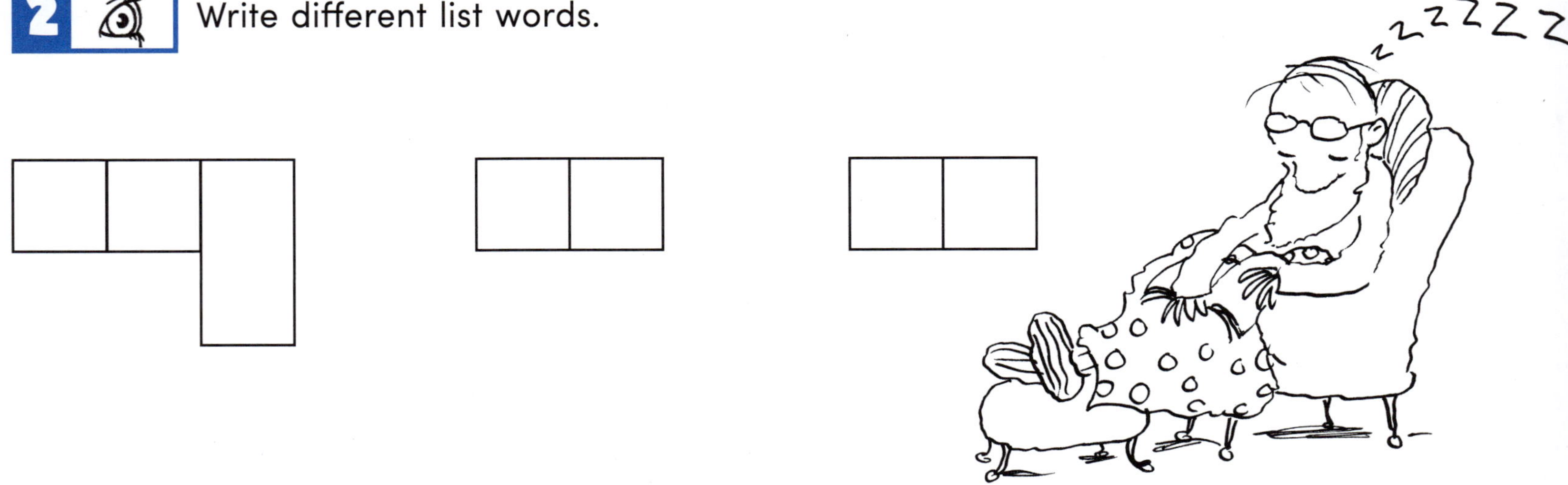

Spelling Rules! Student Book F (ISBN 9780655092667) © Janelle Ho, Helen Pearson

3 Make words with the same first sound.

a < s ______ m ______

n < ip ______ ap ______

4 Write the word from back to front to make a list word.

pan ______ on ______

pin ______ lap ______

Most words add **s** to show there is more than one.

cat → cats *dog → dogs*

5 Add **s** to show more than one.

2 mat __

3 friend __

4 cup __

5 rat __

My own words

______ ______ ______

______ ______ ______

Unit 9

Find a hidden o.

tin	not	got
pot	**log**	**nod**
dot	pod	so

Write the letter that makes the last sound.

 ___

 ___

 ___

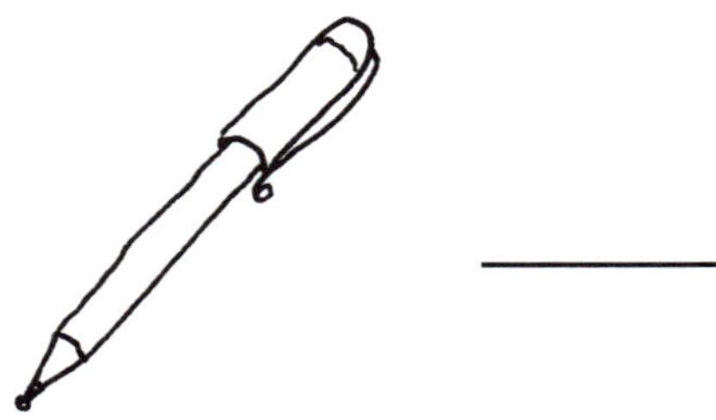 ___

 ___

 ___

Write a list word that rhymes.

pot _ _ _　　nod _ _ _　　no _ _

Spelling Rules! Student Book F (ISBN 9780655092667) © Janelle Ho, Helen Pearson

Make words with different last sounds.

no < d ______ / t ______

do < t ______ / g ______

Write words that match the pictures.

Do n _ _ pat

the d _ _ .

Do n _ _ put a hot

p _ _ o _ the table.

Do n _ _ s _ t on

the l _ g.

My own words

______ ______ ______

______ ______ ______

Unit 10 Revision

Find a hidden c.

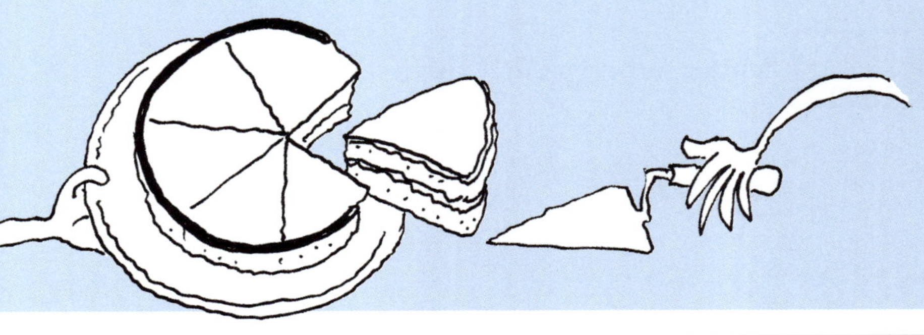

pin	lid	dad

can	man	sad

tan	pop	I

1 Write list words.

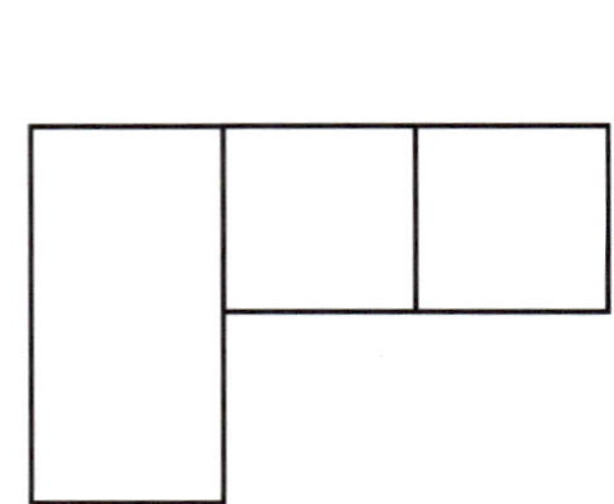
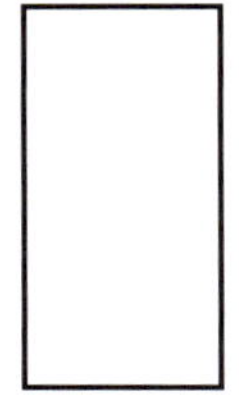
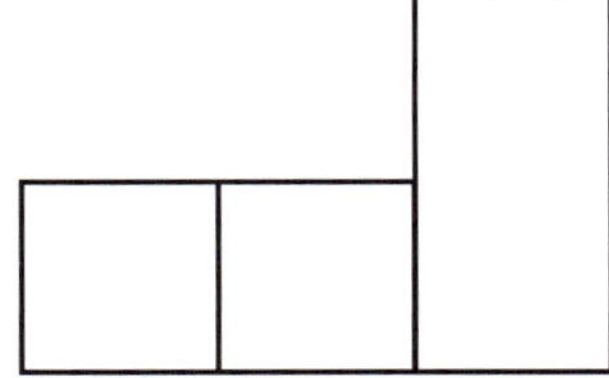
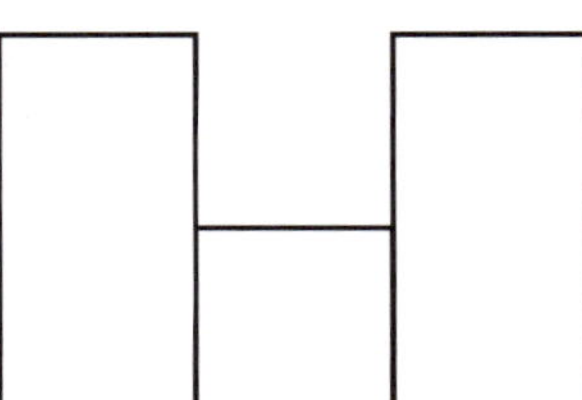

2 Write list words.

_ _ _

_ _ _

_ _ _

3 Write **can** if you can do each thing.

I ______ read a book.

I ______ hit a ball.

I ______ draw a cat.

I ______ cook rice.

4 Write a word you have learned.

a feeling ________

a person ________

a sound ________

a friend ________

a pet ________

5 Write **a**, **i** or **o** for the middle sound.

t _ p

s _ t

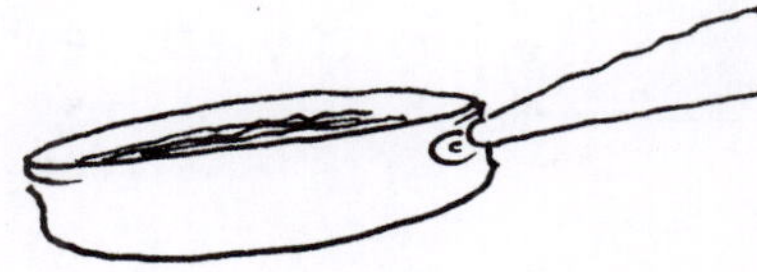

p _ n

l _ d

d _ t

m _ p

My own words

________ ________ ________

________ ________ ________

Unit 11

bat	big	bin

rag	rip	rod

rat	bag	bit

1 Draw something else that begins with the same sound.

b		
r	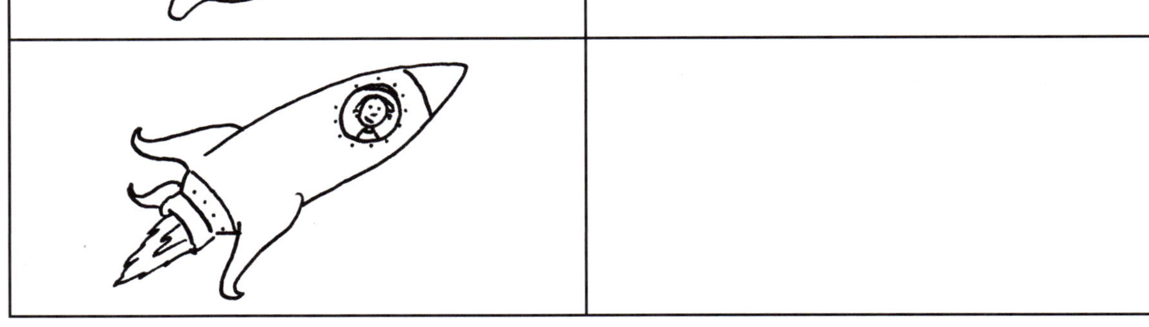	

2 Write the letter that makes the first sound.

 ______  ______ 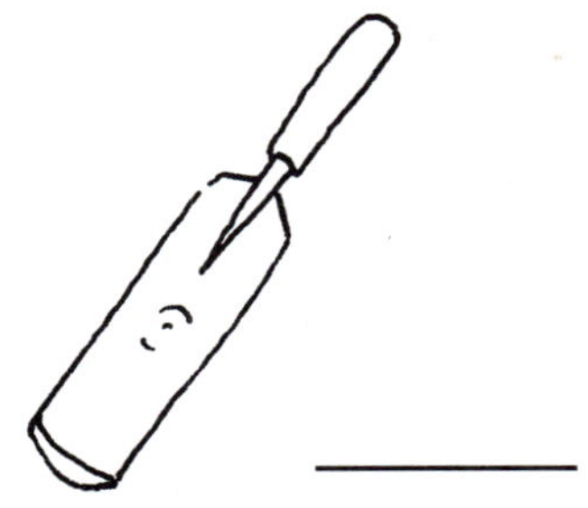 ______

Spelling Rules! Student Book F (ISBN 9780655092667) © Janelle Ho, Helen Pearson

3 Change one letter to make a list word.

nod tin sip bag

_______ _______ _______ _______

4 Look at the picture and finish the sentence.

Pia has a r _ _.

5 Arrange the letters to make a word.

tba _______

gib _______

abg _______

rdo _______

6 Write words that rhyme.

pig

____

____

mat

____

____

rag

____

____

My own words

_______ _______ _______

_______ _______ _______

Unit 12

Find a hidden **e**.

has	**h**ad	an

hat	**h**ot	**e**gg

he	she	me

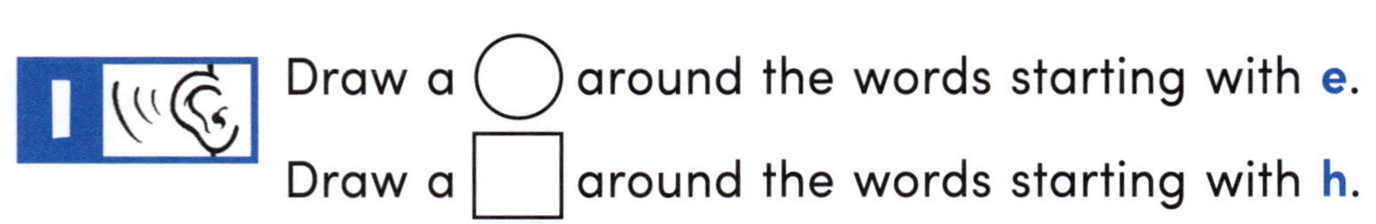

1 Draw a ◯ around the words starting with **e**.

Draw a ☐ around the words starting with **h**.

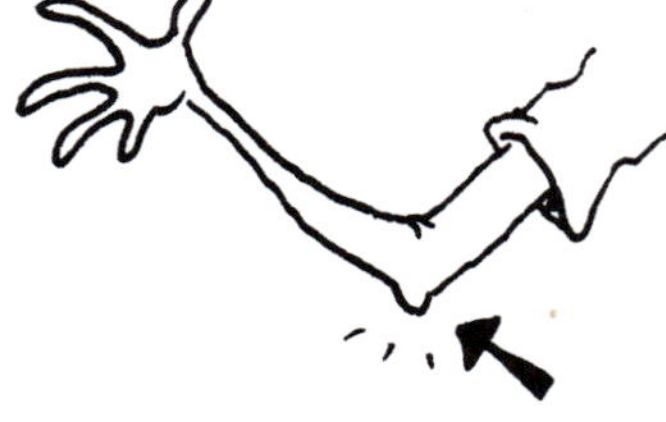

2 Make words with different sounds.

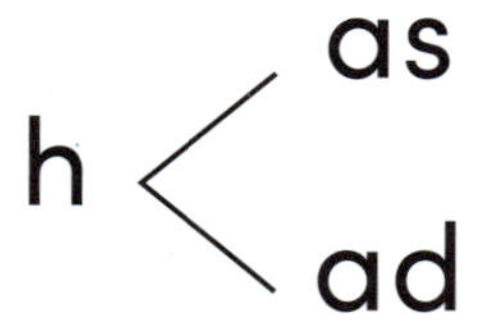

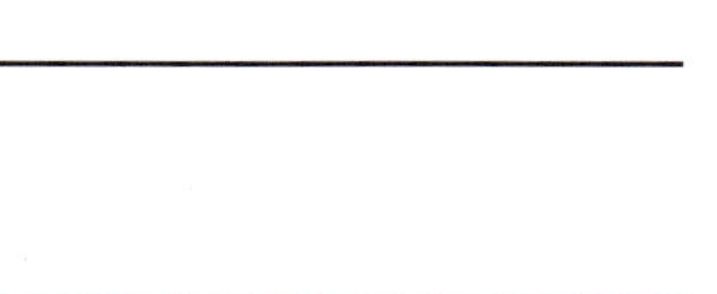

h < as ________ / ad ________

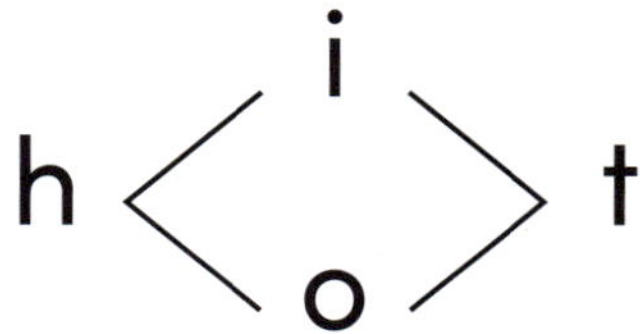

h < i / o > t ________ / ________

an goes before **a**, **e**, **i**, **o**, **u**.
a goes before other letters.

3 Write **a** or **an** for each picture.

______ ______ ______

______ ______ ______

4 Circle the letter that makes the first sound.

e h n    h e a    e a h

5 Write list words.

When it is _ _ _, Pat wears a _ _ _.

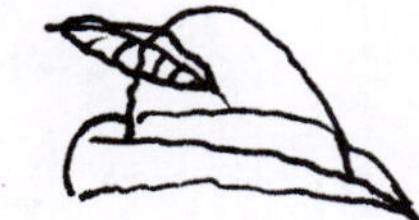

Sam _ _ _ an  _ _ _. He gave it to _ _.

My own words

______ ______ ______

______ ______ ______

Unit 13

Find a hidden **b**.

red	bed	ten

get	pet	mob

him	my	by

1 Colour the ○ if you hear **b** as the first sound.
Colour the □ if you hear **b** as the last sound.

○ □ ○ □

○ □ ○ □

2 Write list words that rhyme.

pen ________ set ________ ________

rob ________ led ________ ________

Spelling Rules! Student Book F (ISBN 9780655092667) © Janelle Ho, Helen Pearson

3  Write list words.

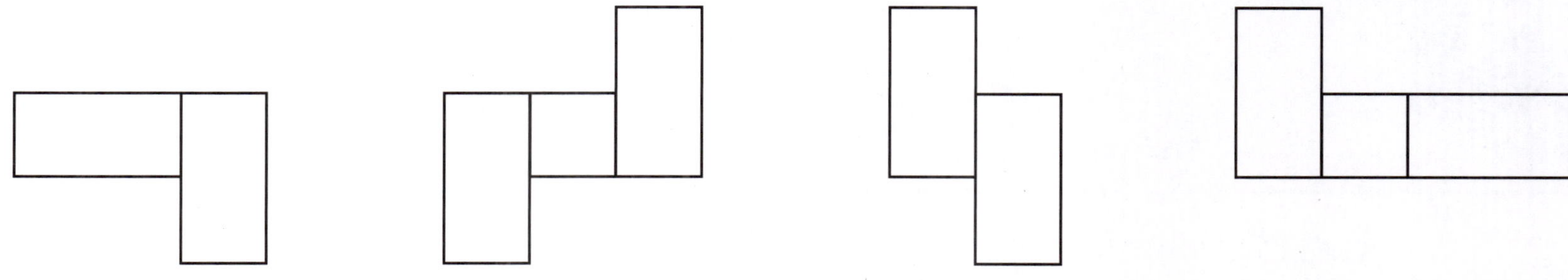

4  Write list words.

'It's time to _ _ _ to _ _ _!' said Mum.

There are _ _ _ pens in _ _ bag.

Dan has a dog for a _ _ _.

5 Colour the shapes with **e** red.

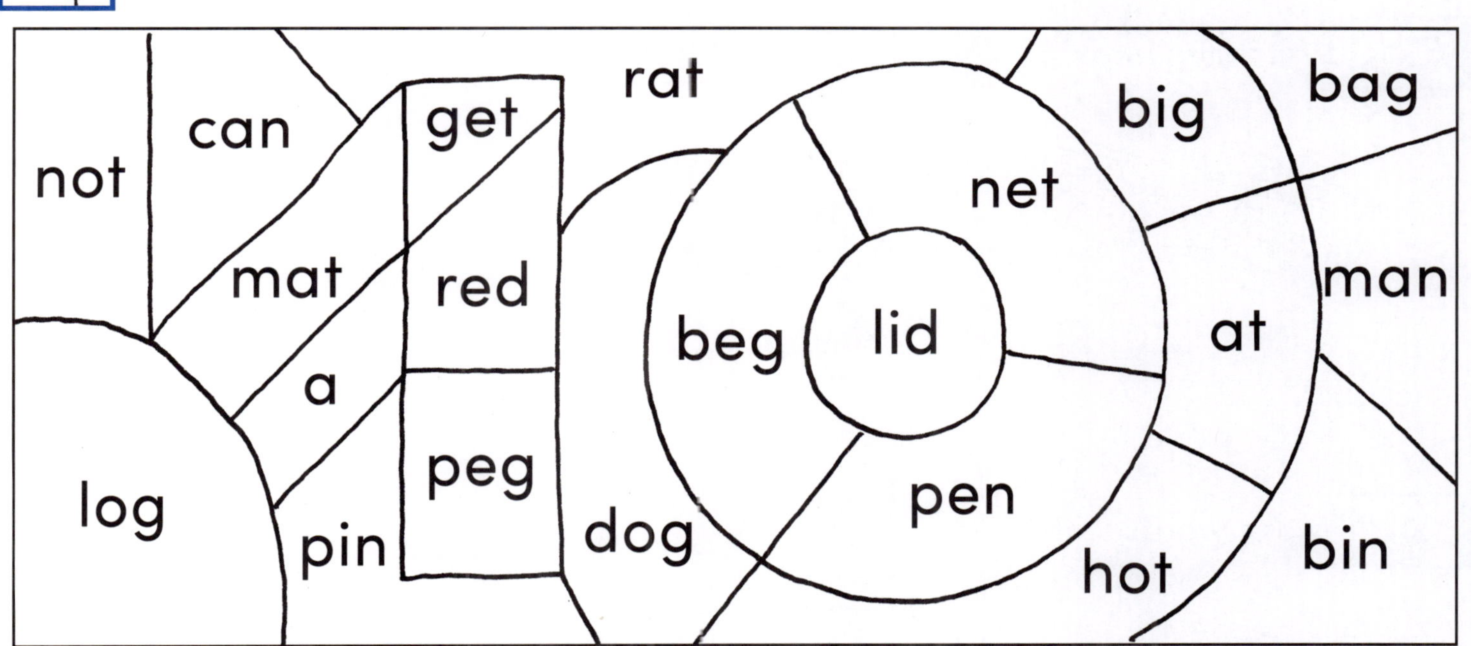

My own words

_______________ _______________ _______________

_______________ _______________ _______________

Unit
14
Revision

bad	net	top

his	hid	hit

her	men	new

 Write list words.

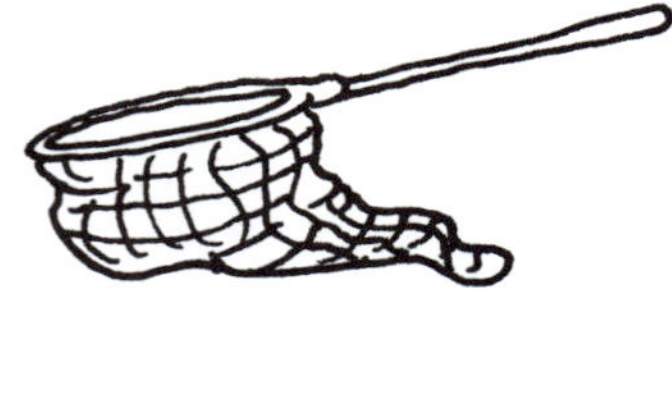

2 Make words with these letters.

b < e / a > d

h < i / a > d

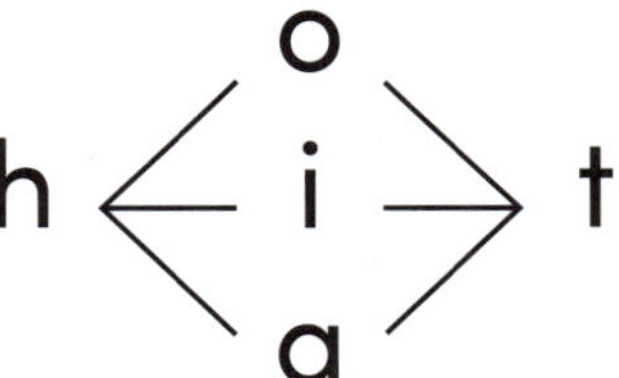

h < o / i / a > t

Spelling Rules! Student Book F (ISBN 9780655092667) © Janelle Ho, Helen Pearson

Write the letter that makes the first sound. Cross out the picture that does not belong.

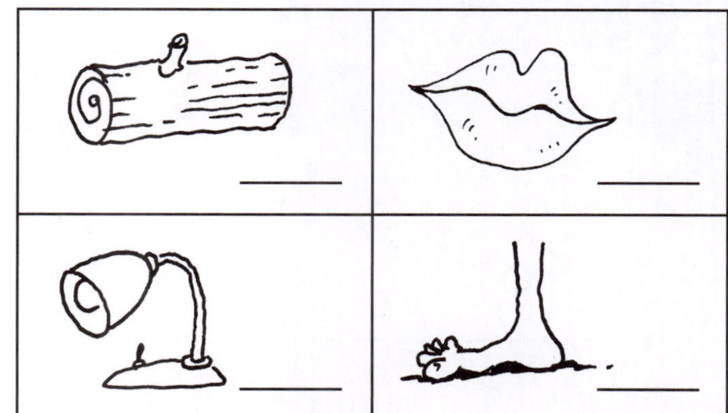

Write to show more than one.

2 _ _ _ _ 3 _ _ _ _ 4 _ _ _ _

Write list words.

Ben took _ _ _ sister's bat. Then he hid _ _ _ ball.

Did she get mad? Yes, she did as they were _ _ _.

Write a list word for each clue.

not good = ________ not bottom = ________

not him = ________ not old = ________

My own words

________ ________ ________

________ ________ ________

Unit 15

Find a hidden **u**.

fat	fan	fin

fit	up	us

or	one	fog

1 Draw something else that begins with the same sound.

f

u

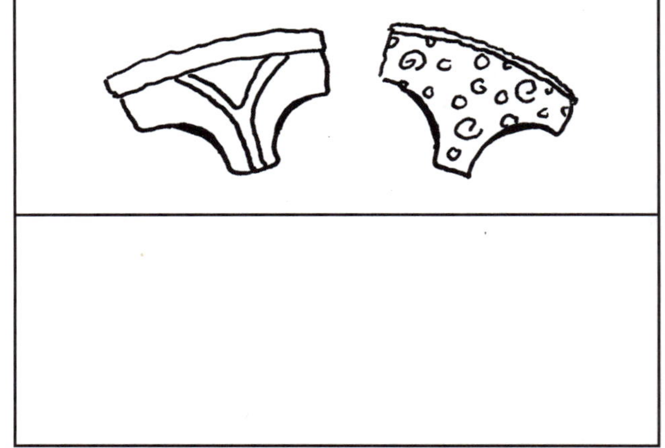

2 Write a list word that has the small word in it.

an	in	on	it
________	________	________	________

Spelling Rules! Student Book F (ISBN 9780655092667) © Janelle Ho, Helen Pearson

3 Write list words.

Ron has ☐☐☐ ☐☐☐ cat.

My fish has a red ☐☐☐.

'Wake ☐☐ !' Rita's mother said.

4 Write **he** or **she** and a list word.

My uncle says _ _ wants to give _ _ a dog.

Ann says _ _ _ wants a pig _ _ a dingo.

5 Write list words.

down ________ ________ thin

My own words

________ ________ ________

________ ________ ________

Unit 16

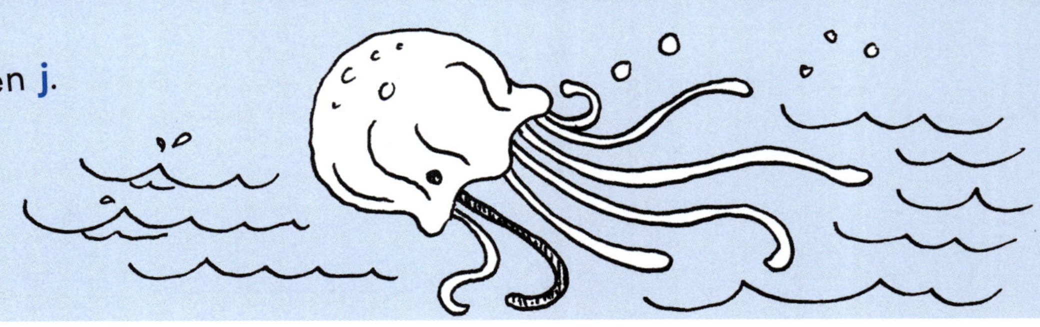

jam	jog	job

be	we	the

to	go	are

1 Say the words. Circle the pictures that start with j in green. Circle the pictures that start with k in red.

2 Write j or k for the first sound.

____

____

____

Spelling Rules! Student Book F (ISBN 9780655092667) © Janelle Ho, Helen Pearson

3 Circle the pairs of words that rhyme.

the be we

so go to

4 Write list words.

5 Write list words.

My own words

Unit 17

Find a hidden **f**.

of	if	mum

sun	run	bus

fun	hug	put

1 Write the letter that makes the last sound.

 ______

 ______

 ______

2 Colour the shapes with **u**.

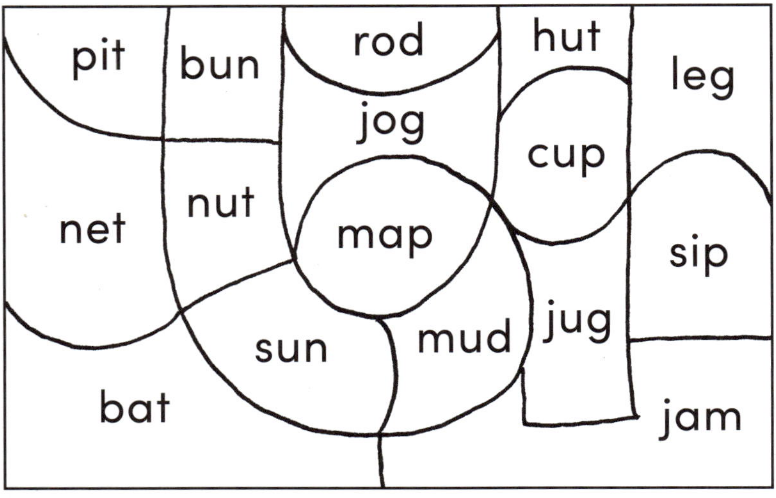

3 Draw the picture.

I give my mum a hug.

Spelling Rules! Student Book F (ISBN 9780655092667) © Janelle Ho, Helen Pearson

Change the vowel to **u** to make a new word.

fan pot beg bin

__________ __________ __________ __________

Write **of**.

a cup _ _ nuts

a jar _ _ jam

6 Write **if** and a list word.

I will _ _ _ on my cap _ _ it is hot.

The _ _ _ will stop for me _ _ I wave.

My own words

__________ __________ __________

__________ __________ __________

Unit 18 Revision

jug	fed	mad

but	mug	leg

and	said	you

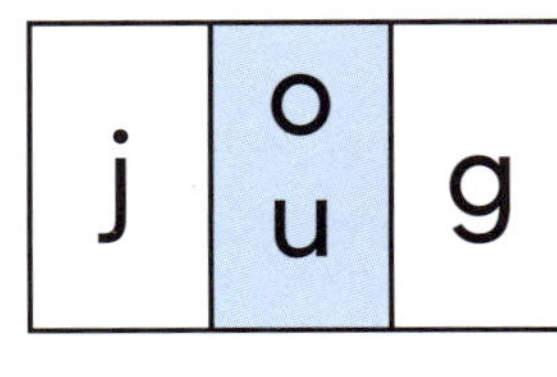

1 Make words with these letters.

b	a e i u	g

b	a e i u	t

j	o u	g

f	e a	d

2 Write a list word that rhymes.

sad

jug

Spelling Rules! Student Book F (ISBN 9780655092667) © Janelle Ho, Helen Pearson

3 Write the letter that makes the first sound.

_ ug   _ ips   _ un

4 Write the letter that makes the last sound.

le _   ca _   co _

5 Write list words.

'Mum _ _ _ _ I must get _ _ _.

Will _ _ _ help me?'

6 Write a word from the box.

and	A rat is big, ________ a pig is bigger.
if	Sip a drink ________ you are hot.
but	Gus has a bat ________ a ball in his bag.

My own words

________ ________ ________

________ ________ ________

Unit 19

Find the hidden a, e, i, o and u.

pan	jet	hip

cob	bug	beg

for	our	out

 Make words with different middle sounds.

a, o, u   c _ t   c _ t   c _ t

e, i, u   b _ g   b _ g   b _ g

 Make words with different first letters.

_ an ______________________   _ ot ______________________

 Make words with different last letters.

pa _ ______________________   hi _ ______________________

Spelling Rules! Student Book F (ISBN 9780655092667) © Janelle Ho, Helen Pearson

4 What letter do you add to show more than one? ____________

5 Write to show more than one.

1 map, 2 ____________ 1 cob, 2 ____________

1 jet, 2 ____________ 1 bug, 2 ____________

6 Say the words. Colour the correct word.

Dad lost | him | his | mug.

I found it for | him | his |.

This gift is | or | for | you.

We went | out | our | to | get | got | the bats.

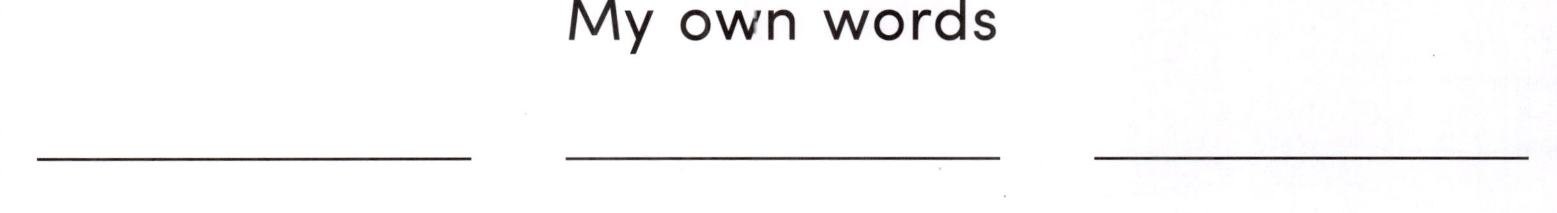

My own words

____________ ____________ ____________

____________ ____________ ____________

Unit 20

Find a hidden **z**.

van	wet	web

yes	zip	zoo

yet	was	will

1 Draw a line to join pictures that start with the same sound.

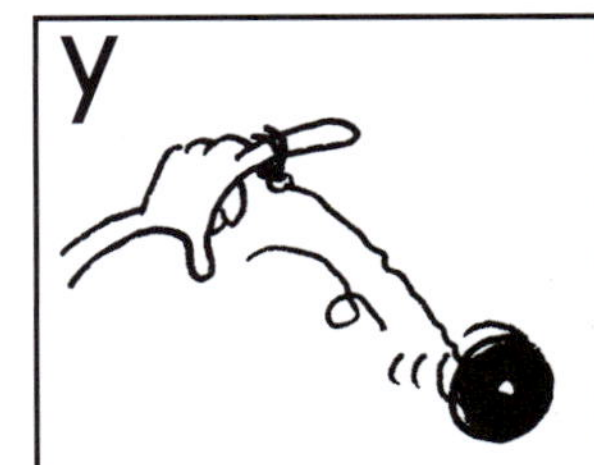

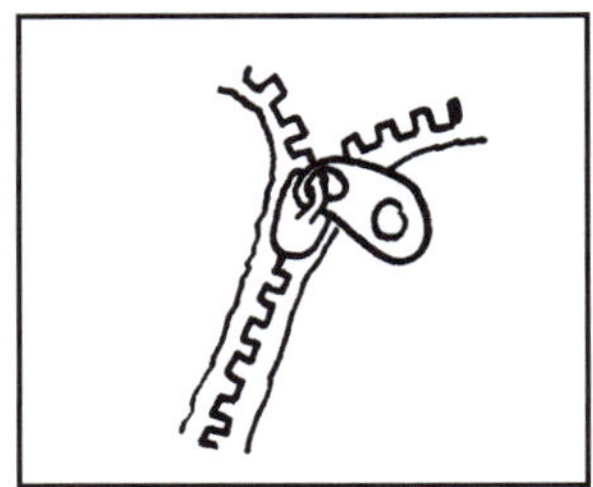

2 Circle the words you see.

y z o o q v a n t n o f z w e t o y e s q u w a s

Spelling Rules! Student Book F (ISBN 9780655092667) © Janelle Ho, Helen Pearson

3 Write list words.

4 Answer the questions. Write **Yes, I do.** or **No, I don't.**

Do you play the violin? ____________________

Do you have a yo-yo? ____________________

5 Finish the question. Use as many list words as you can. Then write an answer.

______ ______ like ______ ? ____________________

6 Write list words.

Jan's dog has a ______ nose.

Mum's old van ______ red.

My own words

______ ______ ______

______ ______ ______

Unit 21

Find a hidden **x**.

six	fix	mix

box	fox	wax

went	very	school

Say the words. Write the first letter.

____ ox

____ ox

____ ix

____ ix

____ ix

Write **go** or **went**.

I ________ to school by bus on Fridays.

Last week after school, I ________ to the park.

Spelling Rules! Student Book F (ISBN 9780655092667) © Janelle Ho, Helen Pearson

 Write the words that rhyme on the same box.

mix	fix	box	six	fox

 Write list words.

Max has ________ socks.

He puts his socks in a ________.

Can you help me ________ my bike?

If you ________ yellow and blue paint, you get green.

Don't tip the candle. The ________ is ________ hot.

My own words

________ ________ ________

________ ________ ________

Unit 22

Find the **A** and the **a** in the bowl of alphabet soup.

1 Write the letters. Write the same letter in lower case.

A ___	B ___	C ___	D ___	E ___
F ___	G ___	H ___	I ___	J ___
K ___	L ___	M ___	N ___	O ___
P ___	Q ___	R ___	S ___	T ___

U ___	V ___	W ___	X ___	Y ___	Z ___

2 Write the missing letters.

a _ c d _ f g _ i j _ l m n o _ q r _ t u _ w _ y z

_ B C _ E F _ H I _ K L _ N _ P _ _ S T _ V

_ X Y _

3 Answer each question.

What are the 5 vowels? _ _ _ _ _

What are the first 3 consonants? _ _ _

4 Finish each sentence.

My name is ______________________________.

My teacher's name is ______________________________.

My friend's name is ______________________________.

My school is called ______________________________.

5 Finish each sentence.

The first letter of the alphabet is ___.

The last letter of the alphabet is ___.

6 Write the letters in alphabetical order.

q t p r s __________ x y w u v __________

i h k l j __________

Unit 23

Find a hidden y.

fry	fly	why

try	cry	sky

this	that	boy

1 Write list words.

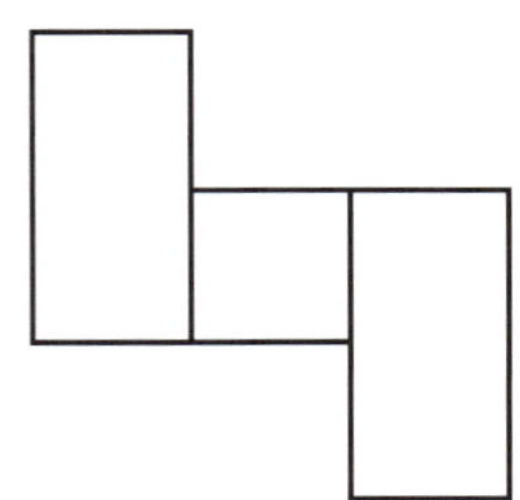

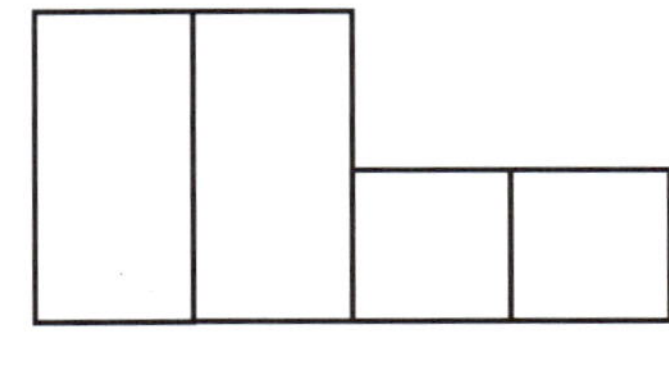

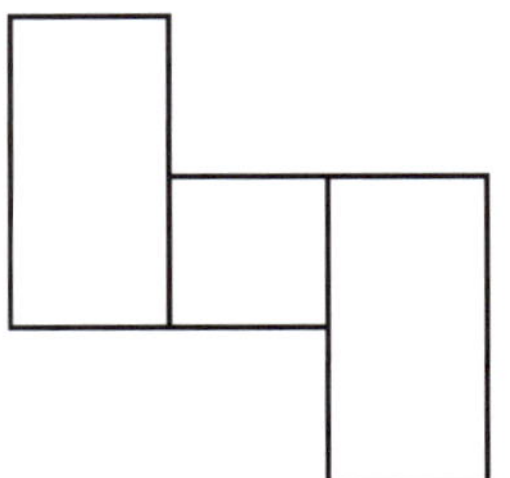

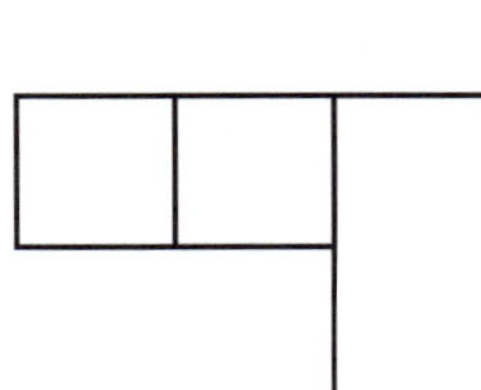

2 Change one letter to make a list word.

t o y   d r y   s t y

________ ________ ________

3 Write a list word.

Question: ________ are dogs like trees?

Answer: They both have barks!

Spelling Rules! Student Book F (ISBN 9780655092667) © Janelle Ho, Helen Pearson

Write the letter **y** to finish the words.

stars in the sk__

birds fl__

fr__ an egg

What are these people saying? Write list words.

2 + 3 =

______ this sum.

Don't ______.

How do birds ______?

A ______ left ______ bag.

My own words

______ ______ ______

______ ______ ______

Unit 24

Find a hidden **s**.

lots	any	many

see	two	how

1 Circle the right word.

bag bags

bat bats

hen hens

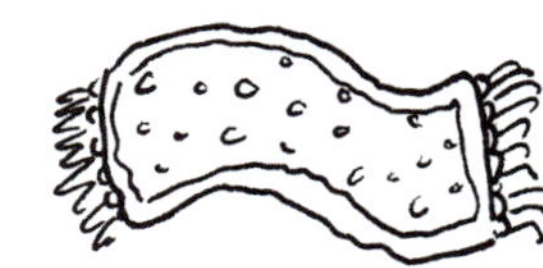

rug rugs

2 Add **s** to show more than one.

2 pig __

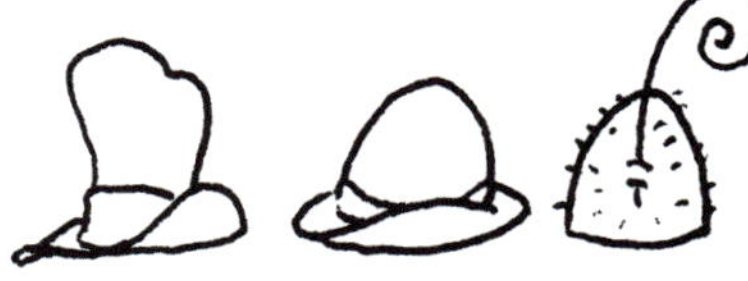

3 hat __

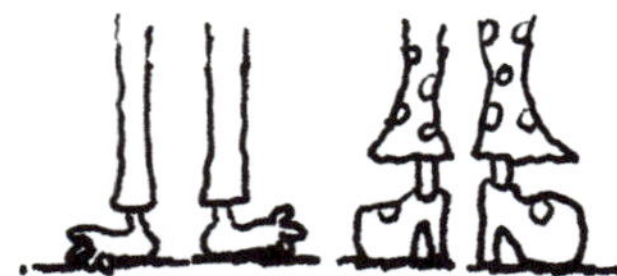

4 leg __

5 ant __

3 Write a sentence for the puzzle.

I 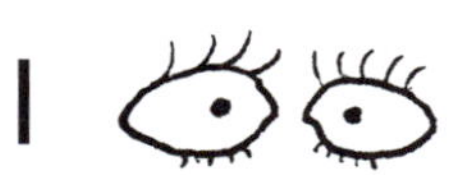 6 

____

____

4 Circle the right word.

Tim has | lots | many | pets.

Dad puts | lots | many | of jam on his toast.

Mum drinks | lots | many | cups of tea.

5 Write **how** and **many**. Then write an answer.

How ________ eggs are in the pan?

There are ________ ________.

________ many cats are on the mat?

There are ________ ________.

________ ________ cups are there?

There are ________ ________.

6 Write the word.

1 ________________ 2 ________________

6 ________________ 10 ________________

My own words

________________ ________________ ________________

________________ ________________ ________________

Spelling Rules! Student Book F (ISBN 9780655092667) © Janelle Ho, Helen Pearson

Write the word that fits the shape.

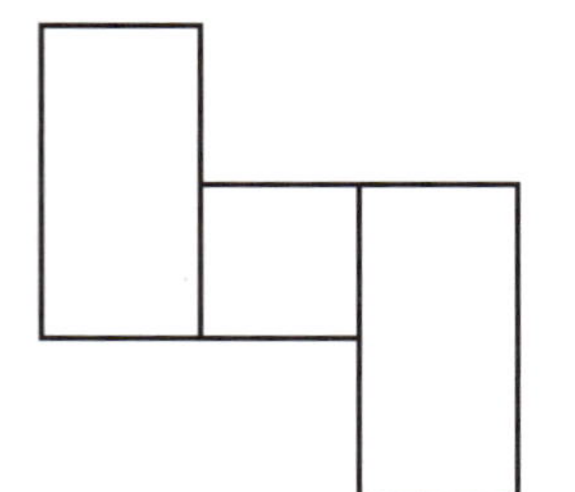

hen
hop
the

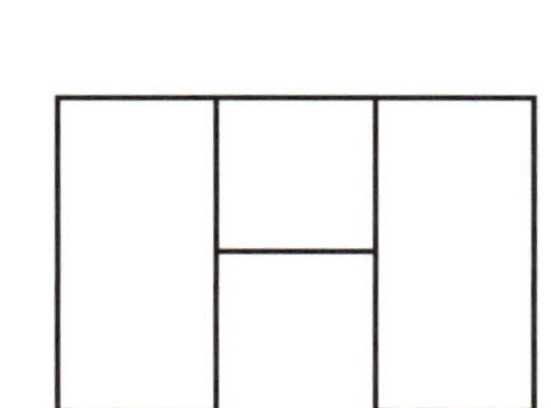

jog
leg
pot

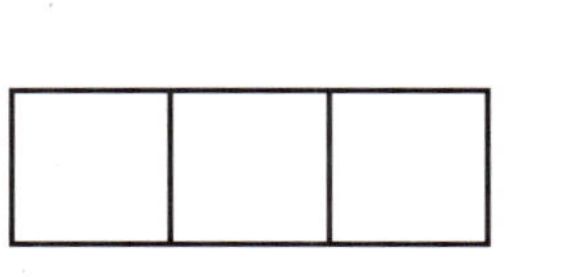

mat
van
ham

Make words with these letters.

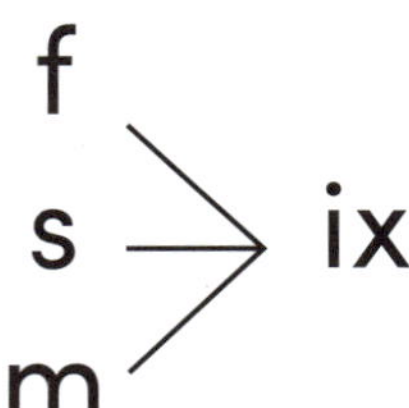

n ← e / o / u → t

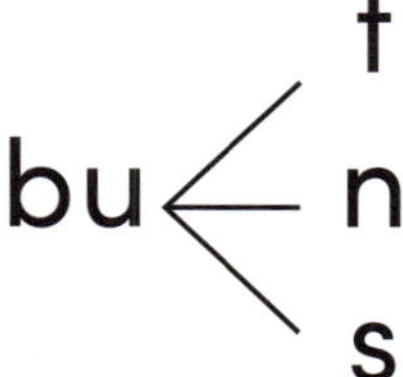

______
______
______

______
______
______

______
______
______

3 Write the word that matches the picture.

wig
dig ______
pig

cry
dry ______
try

fat
fit ______
mat

wet
web ______
rib

Spelling Rules! Student Book F (ISBN 9780655092667) © Janelle Ho, Helen Pearson

Circle the picture that begins with the letter. Write the word.

5 Find ten words in the word worm.

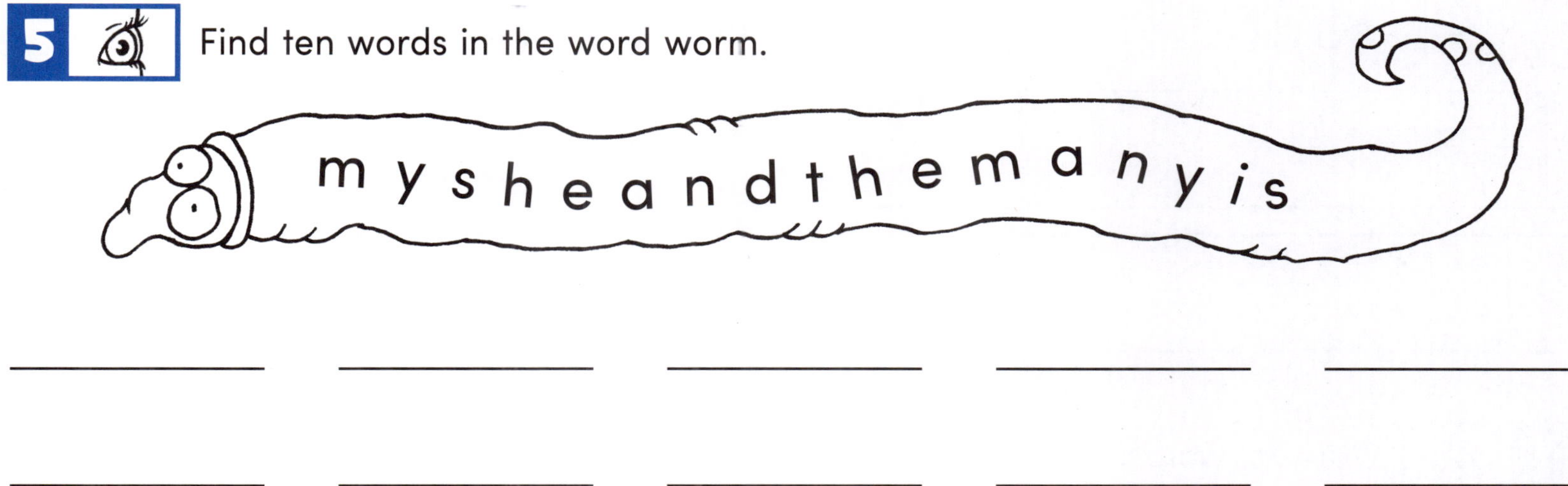

_______ _______ _______ _______ _______

_______ _______ _______ _______ _______

6 Write **and**.

fish _______ chips

pots _______ pans

sun _______ moon

ham _______ eggs

bat _______ ball

cats _______ dogs

My own words

_______ _______ _______

_______ _______ _______

Spelling Rules! Student Book F (ISBN 9780655092667) © Janelle Ho, Helen Pearson

Unit 26

shy	ship	shop

shut	shed	shoe

now	sell	shoes

1 Write list words.

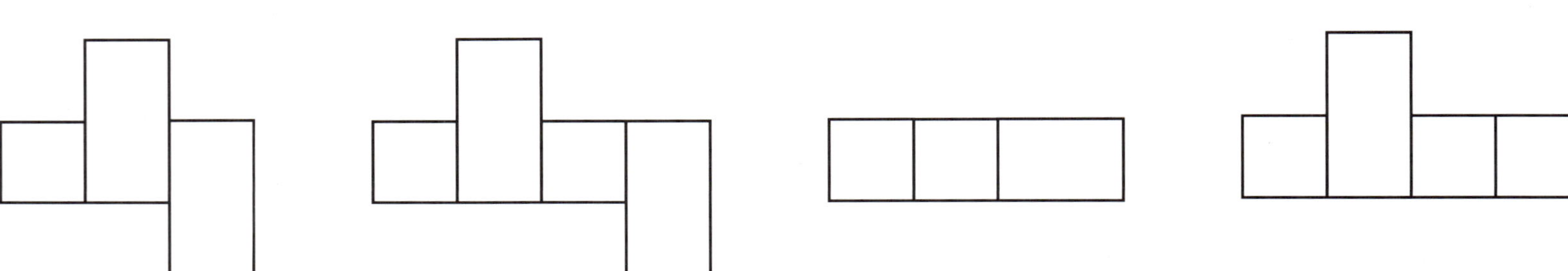

2 The picture shows a small word in the list word. Write the small word.

ship	now	shed	shut
______	______	______	______

Spelling Rules! Student Book F (ISBN 9780655092667) © Janelle Ho, Helen Pearson

 Write list words.

I will put the boxes in the _ _ _ _ _ now.

The new shop sells _ _ _ _ _ _.

Shan is going to Fiji by _ _ _ _ _.

Please _ _ _ _ _ the gate!

A verb adds **s** to show an action happens in the present.

run → runs *hit → hits*

4 Write **s** to show an action happens in the present.

Tim get__ into bed so he can hear a bedtime story.

Jenny shut__ the door to keep the wind out.

This shop sell__ good food.

My own words		
______	______	______
______	______	______

Spelling Rules! Student Book F (ISBN 9780655092667) © Janelle Ho, Helen Pearson

Unit

27

wish	wash	push

fish	cash	rush

want	have	your

1 Say each word. Colour the picture if the word ends in **sh**.

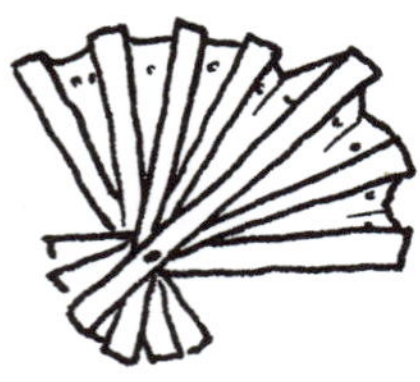   

2 Write list words that have the small word in it.

is	as	us
____________	____________	____________
____________	____________	____________

3 It is your birthday. Write what you wish for.

____

____

Spelling Rules! Student Book F (ISBN 9780655092667) © Janelle Ho, Helen Pearson

4 Write list words.

I do not ________ to go to the shop.

If you ________ the door, it will open.

Shut ________ eyes and make a ________.

5 Draw a picture for the sign.

Wash your hands.

6 Write a list word that has the same middle sound.

fun ________

put ________

van ________

was ________

7 Write a sentence using the word in the box.

have ________

want ________

My own words

________ ________ ________

________ ________ ________

Unit 28

Find a hidden **ck**.

back	duck	neck

sick	shock	quick

were	does	what

Rule **qu** always goes together.

1 Write the missing letters.

_ ueen q _ it _ _ ick

2 Write the middle sound.

d _ ck n _ ck sh _ ck

Spelling Rules! Student Book F (ISBN 9780655092667) © Janelle Ho, Helen Pearson

3 Make words with different first sounds.

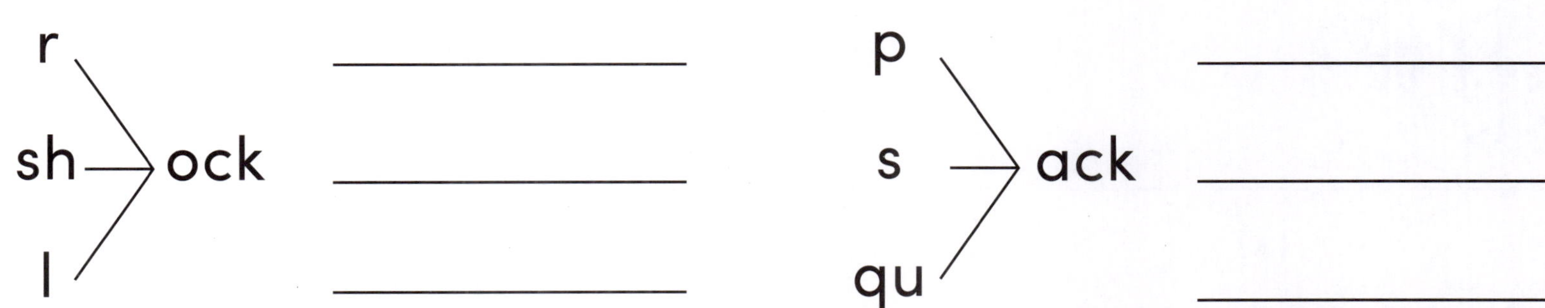

4 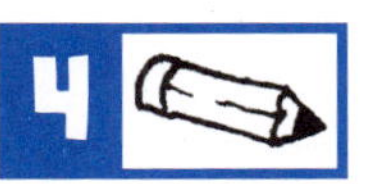 Write list words.

I do not feel well. I am __________.

Dad __________ not like having a bad __________.

5  Write **ck** to answer the riddle.

Guess __________ happened

when the dog ate a clock?

It got a lot of ti __ __ s.

6 Colour the right word.

Rick lost his cat. He | was | were | sad. Jack found it and gave it back. Rick and Jack | was | were | happy.

My own words

__________ __________ __________

__________ __________ __________

Unit 29

Find a hidden ll.

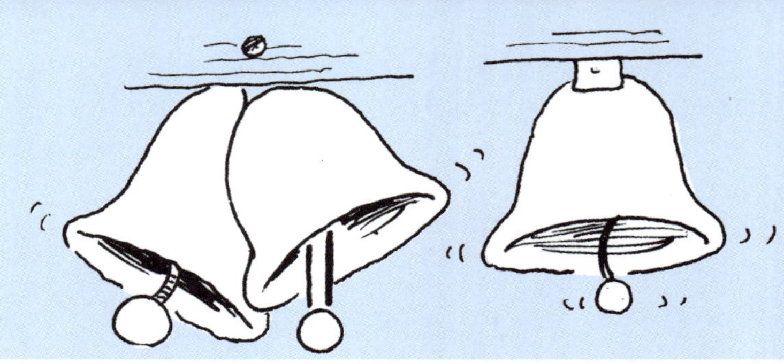

hill	shall	doll

bell	fell	yell

all	call	well

1 Write ll. Draw the picture.

she _ _	do _ _	hi _ _

2 Say the words. Circle the correct word.

Mum | shall | shell | take me to the beach on Sunday.

I like games when we can all | bell | yell | loudly.

Spelling Rules! Student Book F (ISBN 9780655092667) © Janelle Ho, Helen Pearson

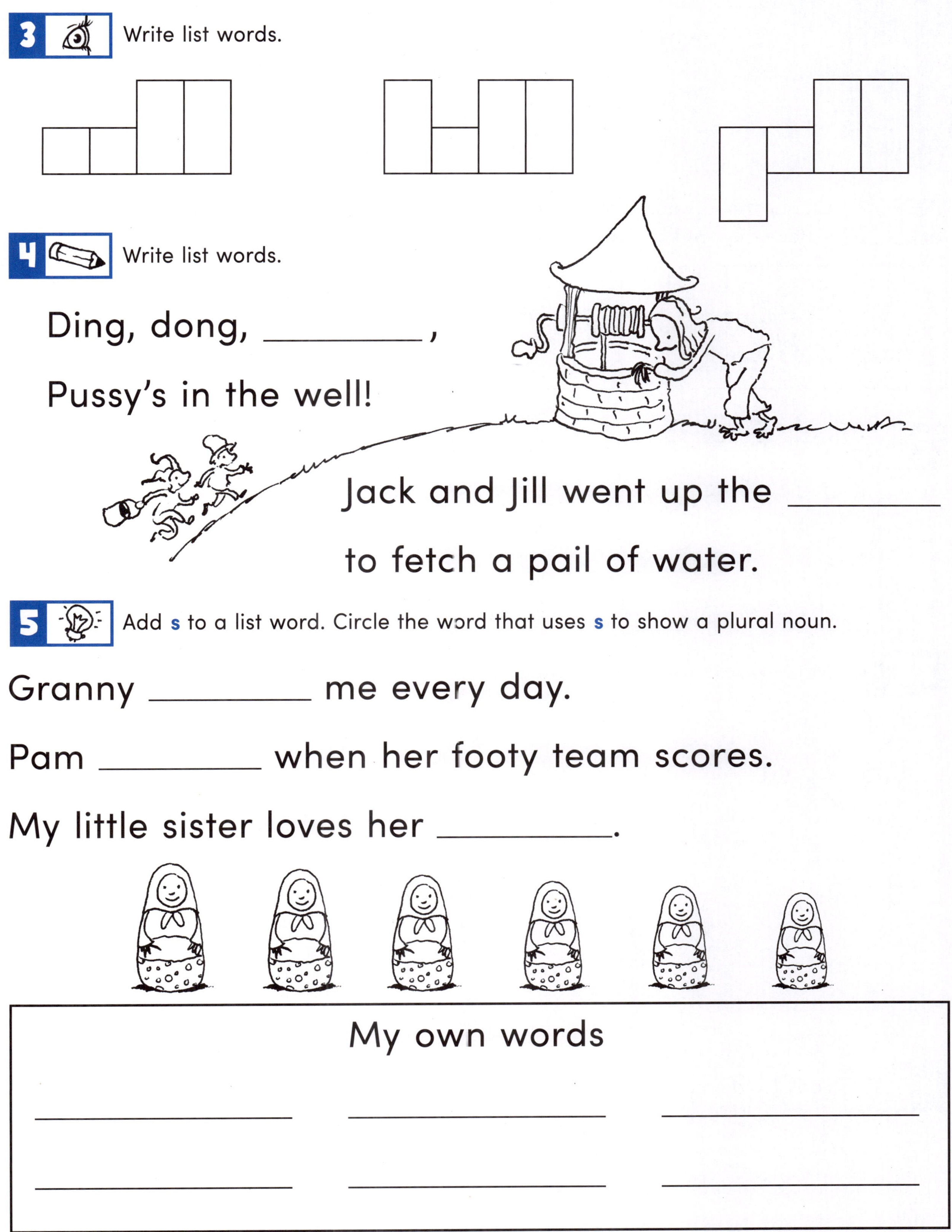

3 Write list words.

4 Write list words.

Ding, dong, ________ ,

Pussy's in the well!

Jack and Jill went up the ________

to fetch a pail of water.

5 Add **s** to a list word. Circle the word that uses **s** to show a plural noun.

Granny ________ me every day.

Pam ________ when her footy team scores.

My little sister loves her ________.

My own words

Unit 30 Revision

Find a hidden **w**.

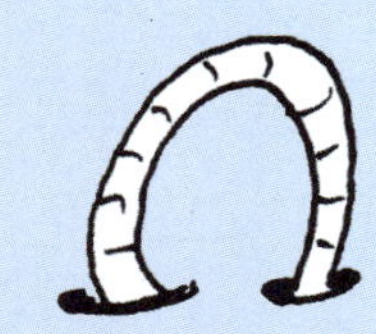
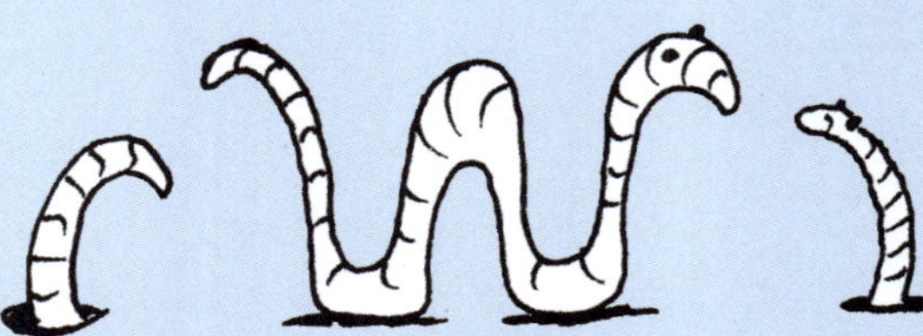

Colour the left box if the sound starts the word.
Colour the right box if the sound ends the word.

Write the letter that makes the middle sound.

Make words with these letters.

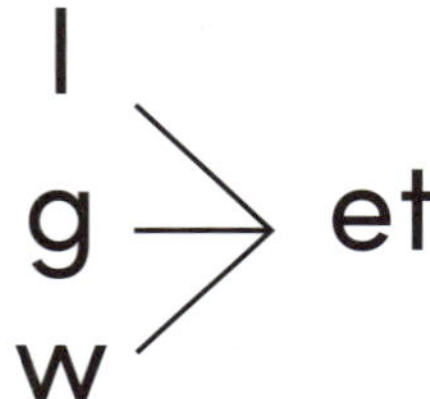

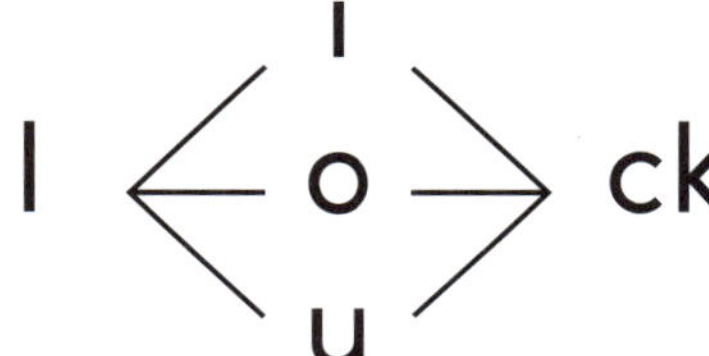

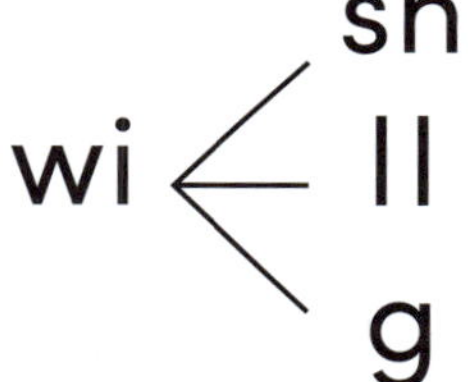

4 Look for a small word inside each word. Write the small word.

hill dish shut bats

Spelling Rules! Student Book F (ISBN 9780655092667) © Janelle Ho, Helen Pearson

Change one letter to make a new word.

log ________ well ________ shy ________

Write the word for each picture.

_ _ _	_ _ _	_ _ _	_ _ _ _

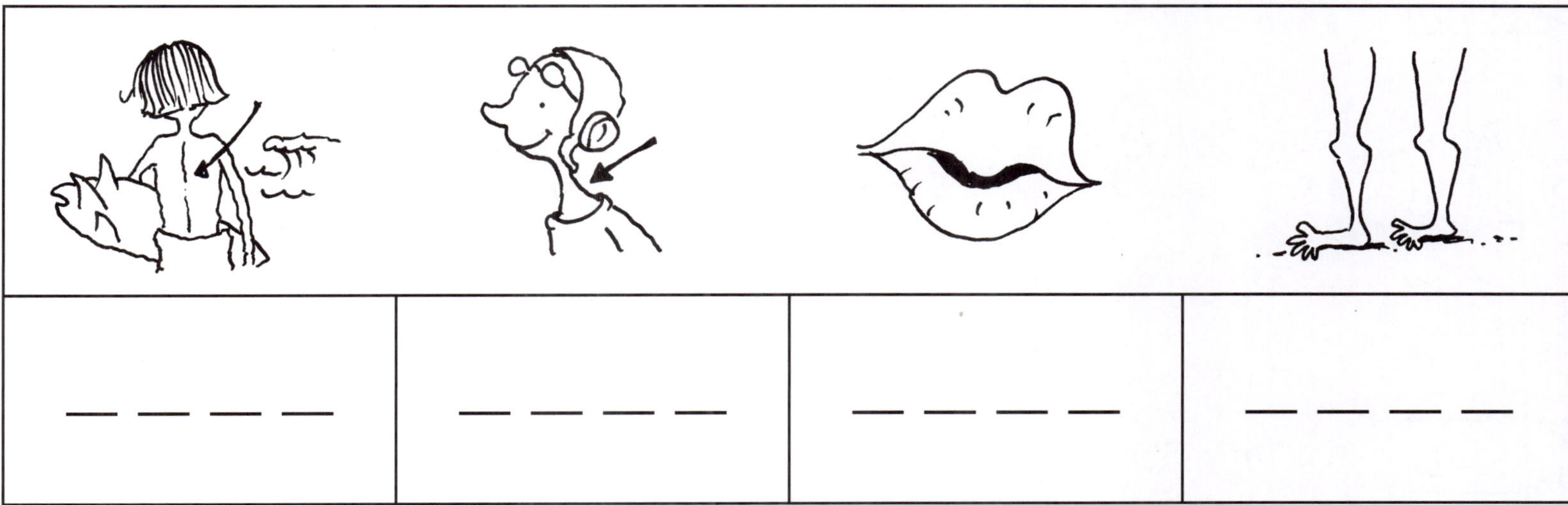

_ _ _ _ _	_ _ _ _ _	_ _ _ _ _	_ _ _ _ _

My own words

________ ________ ________

________ ________ ________

Unit 31

Find a hidden th.

then	them	they

thin	thick	three

four	here	when

 Write sh or th to show the first sound.

______ ______ ______ ______ ______

2 Write They, She or He.

This is Tim. ______ is six.

I see Amit and Lil. ______ have good seats.

Nina is over there. ______ looks ill.

Look at Tess and Finn. ______ can run so fast!

Spelling Rules! Student Book F (ISBN 9780655092667) © Janelle Ho, Helen Pearson

3 Write list words.

I went to the park. ________ I went to the shops.

________ does school end? It ends at 3 o'clock.

The children are having fun. Look at ________.

One, two, ________, ________.

Tip Sentences need spaces between each word.

4 Write each sentence with a space between each word.

Theywenttothepetshop.

____

Canyouseetheminthere?

____

Heretheyare! ________________________________

5 Make a new word by adding **t** or **th** at the beginning.

hat ________	hen ________	is ________
here ________	in ________	his ________

My own words

________ ________ ________

________ ________ ________

Spelling Rules! Student Book F (ISBN 9780655092667) © Janelle Ho, Helen Pearson

Unit 32

Find a hidden **th**.

with	bath	both

moth	path	tooth

good	some	where

Colour 1 if **th** is the first sound.
Colour 2 if **th** is the middle sound.
Colour 3 if **th** is the last sound.

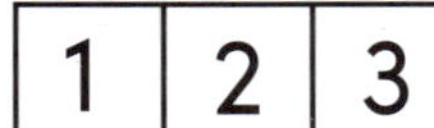

1 2 3 | 1 2 3 | 1 2 3 | 1 2 3 | 1 2 3

The vowels **a**, **i** or **o** have been left out of these words. Write the words with the missing vowel.

bth ________ mth ________ bth ________

pth ________ wth ________ tth ________

3 Write a list word that has the small word in it.

it ________ go ________ so ________ her ________

Spelling Rules! Student Book F (ISBN 9780655092667) © Janelle Ho, Helen Pearson

4 Write list words.

__________ is Dad? He is in the bathroom.

A __________ has four wings so it can fly.

Walk on the __________ and not in the mud.

5 Circle the right word.

Rex hugs | both | bath | his mum and dad. He wants to be | bad | good | to them.

I see | some | any | moths in the web.

Are we | where | there | yet?

6 Finish each sentence to match the picture.

There is ______________________________.

There are two ______________________________.

My own words

__________ __________ __________

__________ __________ __________

List words in unit order

Unit 3
pat
sat
tap

Unit 4
cat
cap
gap

Unit 5
mat
map
it
is
sip
pit
in
a

Unit 6
sit
pig
tip
tag
am
at

Unit 7
dig
lip
lap
dip
do
did

Unit 8
no
nap
nip
as
on
pal
cats
dogs

Unit 9
tin
not
got
pot
log
nod
dot
pod
so

Unit 10
pin
lid
dad
can
man
sad
tan
pop
I

Unit 11
bat
big
bin
rag
rip
rod
rat
bag
bit

Unit 12
has
had
an
hat
hot
egg
he
she
me

Unit 13
red
bed
ten
get
pet
mob
him
my
by

Unit 14
bad
net
top
his
hid
hit
her
men
new

Unit 15
fat
fan
fin
fit
up
us
or
one
fog

Unit 16
jam
jog
job
be
we
the
to
go
are

Unit 17
of
if
mum
sun
run
bus
fun
hug
put

Unit 18
jug
fed
mad
but
mug
leg
and
said
you

Unit 19
pan
jet
hip
cob
bug
beg
for
our
out

Unit 20
van
wet
web
yes
zip
zoo
yet
was
will

Unit 21
six
fix
mix
box
fox
wax
went
very
school

Unit 23
fry
fly
why
try
cry
sky
this
that
boy

Unit 24
lots
any
many
see
two
how

Unit 26
shy
ship
shop
shut
shed
shoe
now
sell
shoes

Unit 27
wish
wash
push
fish
cash
rush
want
have
your

Unit 28
back
duck
neck
sick
shock
quick
were
does
what

Unit 29
hill
shall
doll
bell
fell
yell
all
call
well

Unit 31
then
them
they
thin
thick
three
four
here
when

Unit 32
with
bath
both
moth
path
tooth
good
some
where